*The Call
of the Coast*

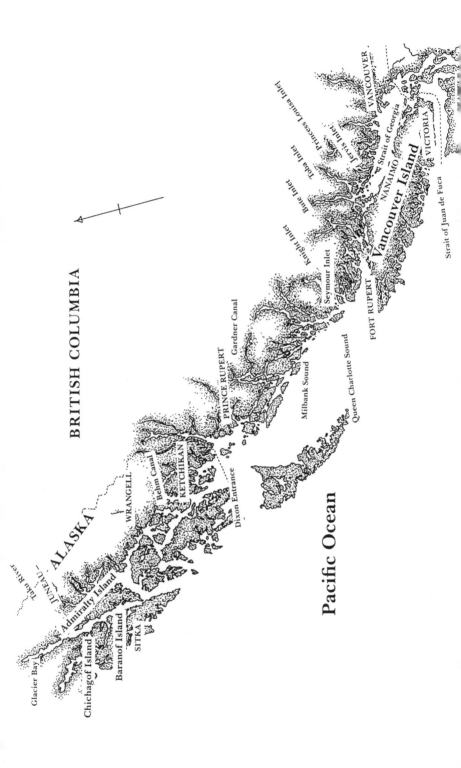

BRITISH COLUMBIA

ALASKA

JUNEAU

Taku River

Glacier Bay

Chichagof Island

Admiralty Island

Baranof Island

SITKA

WRANGELL

Behm Canal

KETCHIKAN

Dixon Entrance

PRINCE RUPERT

Gardner Canal

Milbank Sound

Queen Charlotte Sound

Knight Inlet

Seymour Inlet

Bute Inlet

Toba Inlet

Princess Louisa Inlet

Jervis Inlet

FORT RUPERT

Vancouver Island

NANAIMO

Strait of Georgia

VANCOUVER

VICTORIA

Strait of Juan de Fuca

Pacific Ocean

The Call
of the Coast

compiled and edited by
Charles Lillard

Horsdal & Schubart

Horsdal & Schubart Publishers Ltd.
4252 Commerce Circle
Victoria, BC
V8Z 4M2

Cover painting "Gabriola", by Carol Evans, Dayspring Studio, Fulford Harbour, BC.
Map by Suzanne Prendergast, Ganges, BC, for *Three's a Crew*, by Kathrene Pinkerton (Horsdal & Schubart, 1991).
Drawings by Suzanne Prendergast, Ganges, BC.
Production editing by Rick Behnke.
Cover type by Trade Typesetting, Victoria, BC.
This book is set in Palatino. Printed and bound in Canada by Kromar Printing Ltd., Winnipeg, Manitoba.

For Eric Forrer — Seattle-Vancouver-Victoria-Ketchikan-Juneau...

Canadian Cataloguing in Publication Data

Main entry under title

The Call of the Coast

ISBN 0-920663-14-1

1. Northwest Coast of North America — Description and travel
2. British Columbia — Description 3. Alaska — Description
I. Title II. Lillard, Charles, 1944-

F852.L36 1992 917.87'0162 C92-105672-2

CONTENTS

INTRODUCTION

by Charles Lillard

Travel the Inside Passage and you will never forget the journey. Travel portions of it in a small boat, by yourself, in all weathers; sleep in abandoned Indian villages, dream yourself back into the time when the Tlingit encountered the first Europeans to reach these shores—the Ghostland People—and love every moment of your life there; then there will be those moments...

Sometimes these are nothing more than a remembered gesture; a face hidden away in one of Bill Reid's carvings that makes the hair on my neck rise; come fall it's the wind, the way the wind bowled through the island passes one morning and how, on waking, we knew it was time to move on. The oldest moments return late at night—Richard Brautigan maundering on about the silver stairs of Ketchikan; the sound of black rain on white current where the tide meets fresh water in Rivers Inlet; Rolfe telling me how he rowed from Prince Rupert to Craig, towing a 30-foot hulk all the way...

Who he was he never bothered to say. In his stories he called himself Rolfe, always with something like amusement. Or amazement. He was as unique then as the space we shared is now.

It was twilight when he brought his skiff into that Cat Island beach. "You're cooking salmon the old way," he'd say later. "That's what called me in." It probably did, too. A little man with huge hands, that was my first impression. Maybe his eyes were so close-set there was hardly room for his nose, but his was the biggest damn grin I'd ever seen. He helped himself to the coffee, rolled a cigarette, and started talking.

Little of it made sense at first. He didn't talk, he thought aloud. Once I grasped that, listening was easier. I told Rolfe I was headed south to the islands around the mouth of Portland Canal; his reply sounded something like this:

"Tongass...the Klingeets love it, even having us Yanks nearby at... well, you got to understand..." Here he paused to dip into his gaping shirt pocket and lift out a can of Prince Albert. "Maybe it doesn't bother them. They've known the Ruskies (counting them they ate, Chirikov's boys) for years, ever since the 1740s. Stewed Muscovites, heh-heh-heh. The Ruskies—well..." Slowly he examined his fresh-made cigarette, searched his pockets for a match, and, finding one, struck it on the leg of his overall. Exhaling, he leaned towards me; speaking softly, confidentially, he said, "Maybe Ruskies, more likely siwooshes—left their name there, that's where the Birdmen went after their fight with the dog Wolves."

On it rolled, an eerie river of sound. Rolfe was a man desperate to say the right, real thing. Coffee. Cigarettes. Coast lore years wide and a lifetime deep. He knew one way of life, his own, and one piece of territory, the coast.

Of all the things he told me that night, the poetry of one comment made it indelible; skookum in its simplicity. "Red, all this, why, it's a great river north."

Little wonder that when asked to write a paper on an original metaphor some years later as part of a course requirement, I thought Rolfe's was perfect. "Colorful" wrote the professor at the top of my paper, "but metaphor should expand our thinking."

Pshaw. That learned man hadn't sat on a beach, caught up in a river of sound and time; hadn't descended into the reverie behind the metaphor; couldn't know Rolfe's river rises from the geography and history of the Pacific Northwest, and flows north until it debouches into the ranges that give birth to the Mackenzie and Yukon, two other great rivers north.

Historically this river, the one we call the Inside Passage and what used to be known as the Inland Passage, begins at Nisqually Reach and flows north to Skagway. This makes it a waterway some thousand miles long and frequently no wider than the lower Mississippi. It was a world I fell in love with when I first glimpsed Puget Sound. The love grew in Washington, in Alaska, then in British Columbia; but looking back it was Rolfe, although I was never to meet him again, who was the catalyst. His notion of "a great river north" pulled all the disparate elements of my strange and winding world together. Trying to piece together that riverine story, so I could explain my obsession, first to myself, later to others, led to this gathering, these disparate voices under one cover.

When I met Rolfe almost 40 years ago, there were maybe only a dozen or so coastal books in print. All the books from which the following selections were chosen were unavailable or generally inaccessible to the people to whom they might have meant most. Today there are dozens, maybe scores, of books about the coast in circulation, most of them very good ones, too, and at least one fine coastal magazine. But, and here's the hitch, the literature of our past is still largely unavailable. Of the books represented in this collection, only Grainger's *Woodsmen of the West* (see "The Logging Coast") has been reprinted, so far as is known.

Culturally our riverine world is one of the richest areas in the North American west. It's an exotic world, one with a history and a folklore, with oral and written traditions that are sometimes totally unique; short of somewhat similar inland seas in Europe and Britain, there's nothing like the Inside Passage in the world. This material may be set in a region but it is not regional; here we are dealing with something beyond region, something west of west.

The men and women writing in the following selections were among the first to answer the call of the coast, and here are their responses to the landscape and the figures in the landscape. None of these authors were interviewed about the coast when alive—all the Rolfes must be long dead now—and there is no one else. We must turn to the books by our first authors as we would to a friend's voice. Maybe this will be literature one day; right now most of these men and women sound like ourselves talking. They are worried about work, about no fish next year, logging to excess, and newcomers ruining the country; all are enthralled by the landscape.

If few of these early visitors stayed, the coast worked its magic on them nonetheless. Each of them had to write a book about this new country. Sometimes in their haste these writers got the geography wrong, like Negley Farson's description of the first 25 miles of the Fraser River being in the United States; more often place-names are spelt curiously, though not incorrectly for their day, while others are fictionalized as in Grainger's work. And everyone today knows Lawrence's inaccurate comments about killer whales ("largest and most ferocious known carnivore") are part of our coastal folklore; but does anyone mind? What really matters is that we remember how love drove their pens: that love is part of us now.

Headwaters: The Puget Sound Region

Only the fiords and inlets of the coast of Norway, and the wooded islands in the Inland Sea of Japan present anything like a counterpart to the wonderful scenery of these archipelagoes of the North Pacific.

Eliza Scidmore

ONE

A Cruise on Puget Sound

by Ezra Meeker

So, when we cast off the line at Olympia, on or about the 28th day of May, 1853, we were assured of one thing and that was a concert of action, be there danger or only labor ahead. Neither of us had had much experience in boating, and none as to boat building, but when we decided to make the trip and discarded the idea of taking a canoe we set to work with a hearty good will to build us a skiff out of light lumber, then easily obtained at the Tumwater mill of Hays, Ward & Co., in business at that place.

We determined to have the skiff broad enough to not upset easily, and long enough to carry us and our light cargo of food and bedding. Like the trip across the plains we must provide our own transportation. We were told that the Sound was a solitude so far as transportation facilities, with here and there a vessel loading piles and square timber for the San Francisco market. Not a steamer was then plying on the Sound; not even a sailing craft that essayed to carry passengers. We did not really know whether we would go twenty miles or a hundred; whether we would find small waters or large; straight channels or intricate by-ways; in a word we knew but very little of what lay before us. If we had known a little more, we would not have encountered the risks we did. One thing we knew, we could endure sturdy labor without fatigue, and improvised camp without discomfort, for we were used to just such experiences. Poor innocent souls, we thought we could follow the shore line and thus avoid danger, and perhaps float with the tide, and thus minimize the labor, and yet keep our bearings.

As the tide drew off the placid waters of the bay at Olympia with just a breath of air, our little craft behaved splendidly as the slight ripples were jostled against the bow under the pressure of the sail and brought dreams of a pleasure trip, to make amends for the tiresome pack across the country. Nothing can be more enjoyable than favorable conditions in a boating trip, the more especially to those who have long been in the harness of severe labor, and for a season must enjoy enforced repose. And so we lazily floated with the tide, sometimes taking a few strokes with the oars, and at other times whistling for the wind, as the little town of Olympia to the south became dimmed by distance.

At this southern extremity of the Sound without the accumulations of water to struggle for passage, as through the channel to the north, the movement is neither swift, nor disturbed with cross currents to agitate, the surface more like the steady flow of a great river.

But we were no sooner fairly out of sight of the little village and out of the bay it was situated upon (Budd's Inlet) than the query came up as to which way to go. Was it this channel or that or yet another one we should take? Let the tide decide; that will take us out toward the ocean we urged. No, we are drifting into another bay; that cannot be where we want to go; why, we are drifting right back almost in the same direction from which we came, but into another bay. We'll pull this way to that point to the northeast. But there seems a greater opening of waters to the northwest; yes but I do not see any way out there. Neither is there beyond that point (Johnson's Point); and so we talked and pulled and puzzled until finally it dawned upon us that the tide had turned and we were being carried back to almost the spot from whence we came, into South Bay.

"Now the very best thing we can do is to camp," said the senior of the party of two, to which the junior, your humble writer, readily assented, and so our first night's camp was scarcely twelve miles from where we had started in the morning.

What a nice camping place this. The ladies would say lovely, and why not? A beautiful pebbly beach that extended almost to the water's edge even at low tide with a nice grassy level spit; a back ground of evergreen giant fir timber; such clear cool water gushing out from the bank near by, so superlative in quality as to defy word to adequately describe; and such fuel for the camp fire, broken fir limbs with just enough pitch to make a cheerful blaze and yet body enough to last well.

At the point a little beyond where we landed we found next morning J. R. Johnson, M. D., with his cabin on the point under the pretentious name of "Johnson's Hospital," opened as he said for the benefit of the sick, but, from what I saw in my later trips, his greatest business was in disposing of cheap whisky of which he contributed his share of the patronage.

An Indian encampment being near by, a party of them soon visited our camp and began making signs for trade "*Mika tik-eh clams*" came from out the mouth of one of the matrons of the party as though half choked in the speaking, a cross between a spoken word and a smothered guttural sound in the throat.

"What does she say, Oliver?" the junior said, turning for counsel to the superior wisdom of the elder brother.

"I'm blessed if I know what she says, but she evidently wants to sell some clams."

And so, after considerable dickering, and by signs and gestures and words oft repeated we were able to impart the information that we wanted a lesson in cookery; that we wanted her to "show us how to cook them and that we would buy some." This brought some merriment in the camp. The idea, that there lived a person that did not know how to cook clams. Without saying by your leave or any thing else the motherly looking native began tearing down our camp fire.

"Let her alone," said the senior, "and see what she's up to," noticing that the younger man was going to remonstrate against such an interference with his well laid plans for bread baking. And so the kitchen of the camp was surrendered to the native matron, who quietly covered the hot pebbles and sand where the fire had been, with a light layer of pebbles, upon which the clams were deposited and some fine twigs placed on top, upon which earth was deposited. "K-l-o-o-s-h-e," said the matron. "Hy-as-kloshe," said her seignior, who sat squatting, watching the operation with evident pride upon the achievement of his dame.

"What did they say?" innocently inquired the junior brother.

"I know what they said, but I don't know what they meant," responded the elder one, "unless it was she had done a good job, which I think she has," and thus began and ended our first lesson in the Chinook jargon, and our first introduction to a clam bake.

Our first clam bake gave us great encouragement. We soon learned that these bivalves were to be found in almost unlimited quantity, and were widely distributed; that the harvest was ready twice a day, when the tide was out, and that we need have no fear of a famine even if cast away in some unfrequented place.

"*Yah-ka kloshe al-ta,*" said the dame, uncovering the steaming mass and placing them on a sliver found near by, "*de-late kloshe; kloshe muck-a-muck alt-ta,*"and so, without understanding what she said, but knowing well what she meant, we fell to in disposing of this, our first clam dinner.

Dividing with them the bread that had been baked, and some potatoes that had been boiled, the natives soon withdrew to their own camp, where, before retiring for the night, we repaid the visit.

To see the little fellows of the camp scud behind the mother when the strangers entered, and shyly peep out from their retreat, and the mother lovingly reassuring them with kind, affectionate caresses, and finally coaxing them out from under cover, revealed the character of the natives we had neither of us realized before. We had been in the Indian country for nearly a year, but with guns by our sides if not in our hands for nearly half the time, while on the plains, but we had not stopped to study the Indian character. We took it for granted that the Indians were our enemies and watched them suspiciously accordingly, but here seemed to be a disposition manifested to be neighborly and helpful. We took a lesson in Chinook, and by signs and words combined held conversation until a late hour, when, upon getting ready for taking leave, a slice of venison was handed us, sufficient for several meals. Upon offering

5

to pay for it we were met with a shake of the head, and with the words, *"wake, wake, kul-tus-pot-latch,"* which we understood by their actions to mean they made us a present of it.

This present from the Indian let in a flood of light upon the Indian character. We had made them a present first, it was true but we did not expect any return, except perhaps good will, and in fact, cannot now say we particularly expected that, but were impelled to do our act of courtesy from the manner of their treatment and from the evident desire to be on friendly terms. From that time on during the trip, and I may say, for all time since, I have found the Indians of Puget Sound ready to reciprocate acts of kindness, and hold in high esteem a favor granted if not accompanied by acts apparently designed to simply gain an advantage.

"Keep to the right, as the law directs," is an old western adage that governs travelers on the road, but we kept to the right because we wanted to follow the shore, as we thought it safer, and besides, why not go that way as well as any other,—it was all new to us. So, on the second morning, as we rounded Johnson's Point and saw no channel opening in any direction, saw only water in the foreground and timber beyond, we concluded to skirt the coast line and see what the day would bring forth. This led us a southeasterly course and in part doubling back with that traveled the previous day, and past what became the historic rounds of the Medicine Creek Treaty council, or, rather leaving this two miles to our right, the Nisqually flats were encountered. Here we were crowded to a northerly course leaving the Nisqually House on the beach to the east without stopping for investigation.

According to Finlayson's journal, as I afterwards ascertained, this had been built twenty-three years before. At least some house had been built on this spot at that time, (1829 or 1830) though the fort by that name one fourth mile back from the water was not constructed until the summer of 1833, just twenty years previous to our visit.

This fort mentioned must not be confounded with the Nisqually fort built some three years later (1836) a mile farther east and convenient to the waters of Segwalitchew Creek, which there runs near the surface of the surrounding country. All remains of the old fort have long since vanished, but the nearly filled trenches where the stockade timbers stood can yet be traced, showing that a space 200 feet square had been enclosed.

An interesting feature of the intervening space between the old and the newer fort is the dense growth of fir timber averaging nearly two feet in diameter and in some cases fully three, and over a hundred feet high on what was prairie when the early fort builders began work. The land upon which this timber is growing still shows unmistakable signs of the furrow marks that can be traced through the forest. Verily, this is a most wonderful country where forest product will grow, if properly protected, more rapidly than the hand of man will destroy.

As the tide and wind favored us we did not stop, but had not proceeded far before we came in sight of a fleet of seven vessels lying at anchor in a large bay of several miles in extent.

Upon the eastern slope of the shores of this bay lay the two towns, Port Steilacoom, established January 23rd, 1851, by Captain Lafayette Balch and Steilacoom City, upon an adjoining land claim taken by John B. Chapman, August 23rd, of the same year and later held by his son, John M. Chapman. These two rival towns were built as far apart as possible on the frontage lands of the claim owners (about one mile apart) and became known locally as Upper and Lower Steilacoom, the latter name being applied to Balch's town.

Evidently a far larger trade centered on Steilacoom Bay and vicinity than at any other point we had seen and, as we found afterwards, than any other point on Puget Sound. Naturally we would here call a halt to examine the country and to make ourselves acquainted with the surroundings that made this early center of trade.

One mile and a half back from the shore and east of Lower Steilacoom, we found what was by courtesy called Fort Steilacoom, but which was simply a camp of a company of United States soldiers, in wooden shells of houses and log cabins. This camp, or fort, had been established by Captain Bennett H. Hill with Company M 1st Artillery, August 27th, 1849, following the attempted robbery of Fort Nisqually the previous May by Pat Kanim and his followers, the Snoqualmie Indians.

Dr. Tolmie, Chief Factor of the Puget Sound Agricultural Company at Fort Nisqually, quickly seized the opportunity to demand rent from the United States for the occupancy of the site of Fort Steilacoom of six hundred dollars a year, and actually received it for fifteen years and until the final award was made extinguishing the claims of his company.

It was here, and I think at this time, I saw the Indian "Steilacoom" who still lives. I saw him recently at his camp in the Nisqually bottom, and judge he is bordering on ninety years. Steilacoom helped to build old Fort Nisqually in 1833, and was a married man at that time. People called him chief because he happened to bear the name adopted for the town and creek, but he was not a man of much force of character and not much of a chief. I think this is a remarkable case of longevity for an Indian. As a race, they are short lived. It was here, and during this visit, we began seeing Indians in considerable numbers. Off the mouth of the Nisqually and several places along the beach and floating on the bay we saw several hundred in the aggregate of all ages and kinds. There seemed to be a perfect abandon as to care or thought for the future, or even as to the immediate present, literally floating with the tide.

The gravelly plains near Steilacoom would not do; neither the heavy fir timber lands skirting the waters of the Sound, and we were nonplussed and almost ready to condemn the country. Finally, on the fourth day after a long, wearisome tramp, we cast off at high tide, and in a dead calm, to continue our cruise. The senior soon dropped into a comfortable afternoon nap, leaving me in full command. As the sun shone nice and warm and the tide was taking us rapidly in the direction we wanted to go, why not join, even if we did lose the sight seeing for which the journey was made.

I was shortly after aroused by the senior exclaiming, "What is that?" and then answering half to himself and half to me, "Why, as I live, it's a deer swimming way out here in the bay." Answering, half asleep and half awake, that that could not be, the senior said: "Well, that's what it is." We gave chase and soon succeeded in getting a rope over its horns. We had by this time drifted into the Narrows, and soon found that we had something more important to look after than towing a deer among the tide-rips of the Sound, and turning him loose pulled for dear life for the shore, and found shelter in an eddy. A perpendicular bluff rose from the high water mark, leaving no place for a camp fire or bed. The tide seemed to roll in waves and with contending forces of currents, and counter currents, yet all moving in a general direction. It was our first introduction to a real genuine, live tide-rip, that seemed to harry the waters as if boiling in a veritable caldron, swelling up here and there in centers to whirl in dizzy velocity and at times break into a foam, and, where a light breeze prevailed, into spray. Then in some areas it would seem the waters in solid volume would leap up in conical, or pointed shape—small waves broken into short sections, that would make it quite difficult for a flat bottom boat like our little skiff to float very long. We congratulated ourselves upon the escape, while belittling our careless imitation of the natives of floating with the tide. Just then some Indian canoes passed along moving with the tide. We expected to see them swamped as they encountered the troubled waters, but to our astonishment they passed right through without taking a drop of water. Then here came two well-manned canoes creeping along shore against the tide. I have said well-manned, but in fact, half the paddles were wielded by women, and the post of honor, or that where most dexterity was required, was occupied by a woman. In shore, short eddies would favor the party, to be ended by a severe tug against the stiff current.

By the time the tide had turned, night had come and we were in a quandary as to what to do; whether to camp in our boat, or to start out on unknown waters in the dark. Our Indian visitors began making preparations to proceed on their journey, and assured us it was all right ahead, and offered to show us the way to good camping grounds in a big bay where the current was not strong, and where we would find a great number of Indians in camp.

Sure enough, a short pull with a favorable current brought us through the Narrows and into Commencement Bay and in sight of numerous camp fires in the distance. Our Indian friends lazily paddled along in company, while we labored vigorously with our oars as we were by this time in a mood to find a camp where we could have a fire and prepare some food. I remember that camp quite vividly, though cannot locate it exactly, but know that it was on the water front within the present limits of the City of Tacoma. A beautiful small rivulet came down a ravine and spread out on the beach, and I can remember the shore line was not precipitous and that it was a splendid camping ground. The particular thing I do remember is our supper of fresh salmon. Of all the delicious fish known, give me the salmon caught by trolling in early summer in the deep waters of Puget Sound; so fat that the excess of oil must be turned out of the pan while cooking. We had not then learned the art of cooking on the spit, or at least, did not practice it. We had scarcely gotten our camp fire under way before a salmon was offered us.

We were now in the bay, since made famous in history by that observing traveler, Theodore Winthrop, who came from the north a few months later and saw that great mountain, that "cloud compeller," reflected in the placid waters of the Sound, "Tacoma" as he wrote, Rainier, as we saw it. A beautiful sight it was and is, whatever the name, but to us it was whatever others said it was, while Winthrop, of a poetic mind, was on the alert for something new under the sun, if it be no more than a name for a great mountain.

Winthrop came in September, while we were in the bay in June, thus ante-dating his trip by three months or more. To Winthrop belongs the honor of originating the name Tacoma from some word claimed to have been spoken by the Indians as the name of the mountain. As none of the pioneers ever heard the word until many years afterwards; and not then until after the posthumous publication of Winthrop's works ten years after his visit, I incline to the opinion that Winthrop coined the word out of his imaginative brain.

We again caught sight of the mountain the next day, as we approached the tide flats off the mouth of the Puyallup River. We viewed the mountain with awe and admiration, but gave no special heed to it, more than to many other new scenes engaging our attention. It was land we wanted whereby we might stake a claim, and not scenery to tickle our fancy.

We floated into the mouth of the Puyallup River with a vague feeling as to its value, but did not proceed far until we were interrupted by a solid drift of monster trees and logs, extending from bank to bank up the river for a quarter of a mile or more. We were told by the Indians there were two other like obstructions a few miles farther up the river, and that the current was "*de-late-hyas-skoo-kum*," which interpreted means that the current was very strong. We found this to be literally true during the next two or three days we spent on the river.

We lingered at the mouth of the river in doubt as to what best to do. My thoughts went back to the wife and baby in the lonely cabin on the Columbia River, and then again to that bargain we had made before marriage that we were going to be farmers, and how could we be farmers if we did not have the land? Under the donation act we could hold three hundred and twenty acres, but we must live on it for four years, and so it behooved us to look out and secure our location before the act expired, which would occur the following year. So, with misgivings and doubts, we finally, on the fourth day, loaded our outfit into our skiff and floated out on the receding tide, whither, we did not know.

As we drew off on the tide from the mouth of the Puyallup River, numerous parties of Indians were in sight, some trolling for salmon, with a lone Indian in the bow of his canoe, others with a pole with barbs on two sides fishing for smelt and used in place of a paddle, while again, others with nets, all leisurely pursuing their calling, or more accurately speaking, waiting for a fisherman's luck. Again, other parties were passing, singing a plaintive ditty in minor key with two or more voices, accompanied by heavy strokes of the paddle handle against the side of the canoe as if to keep time. There were really some splendid female voices to be heard, as well as male; and though there were but slight variations in the sounds or words, they seemed never to tire in repeating, and, I must confess, we never tired of listening. Then, at times, a break in the singing would be followed by a hearty laugh, or perhaps a salutation be given in a loud tone to some distant party, which would always bring a response, and with the resumption of the paddles, like the sailors on the block and fall, the song would be renewed, oftentimes to bring back a distant echo from a bold shore. These scenes were repeated time and again, as we encountered the natives in new fields that constantly opened up to our view.

We laid our course in the direction the tide drew us, directly to the north in a channel three miles in width, and discarded the plan of following the shore line, as we found so little variation in the quality of soil. By this time we began to see that opportunities for farms on the immediate shores of Puget Sound were few and far between—in fact, we had seen none. During the afternoon and after

11

we had traveled, by estimate, near twenty miles, we saw ahead of us larger waters, where, by continuing our course, we would be in a bay of five or six miles in width, with no very certain prospect of a camping place. Just then we spied a cluster of cabins and houses on the point to the east, and made a landing at what proved to be Alki Point, the place then bearing the pretentious name of New York.

We were not any too soon in effecting our landing, as the tide had turned and a slight breeze had met it, the two together disturbing the water in a manner to make it uncomfortable for us in our flat bottomed boat.

Here we met the irrepressible C. C. Terry, proprietor of the new townsite, but keenly alive to the importance of adding to the population of his new town. But we were not hunting townsites, and of course lent a deaf ear to the arguments set forth in favor of the place.

Captain William Renton had built some sort of a sawmill here, that laid the foundation to his great fortune accumulated later at Port Blakely, a few miles to the west, to which point he later removed. Terry afterwards gave up the contest, and removed to Seattle.

We soon pushed on over to the east where the steam from a saw-mill served as the guiding star, and landed at a point that cannot have been far removed from the western limit of the present Pioneer Place of Seattle, near where the totem pole now stands.

Here we found the never to be forgotten Yesler, not whittling his pine stick as in later years, but as a wide awake business man, on the alert to drive a trade when an opportunity offered, or spin a yarn, if perchance time would admit. I cannot recall meeting Mr. Denny, though I made his acquaintance soon after at my own cabin on McNeil's Island. In fact we did not stay very long in Seattle, not being very favorably impressed with the place. There was not much of a town, probably twenty cabins in all, with a few newer frame houses. The standing timber could scarcely have been farther removed than to be out of reach of the mill, and of course, scarcely the semblance of a street. The lagoon presented an uninviting appearance and scent, where the process of filling with slabs and saw dust had already begun. The mill, though, infused activity in its immediate vicinity, and was really the life of the place.

As we were not looking for a millsite or a townsite, we pushed on north the next day. We had gone but a few miles until a favorable breeze sprang up, bringing with it visions of a happy time sailing, but with the long stretch of open waters back of us of ten miles or more and of several miles in width, and with no visible shelter ahead of us, or lessening of width of waters, we soon felt the breeze was not so welcome after all. We became doubtful as to the safety of sailing, and were by this time aware of the difficulty of rowing a small, flat bottom boat in rough waters with one oar sometimes in the water and the other in the air, to be suddenly reversed. While the wind was in our favor, yet the boat became almost unmanageable with the oars. The sail once down was not so easy to get up again, with the boat tipping first one way and then another, as she fell off in the trough of the waves. But finally, the sail was set again, and we scudded before the wind at a rapid rate, not feeling sure of our bearings, or what was going to happen. The bay looked to us as if it might be five miles or more wide, and in fact, with the lowering weather, we could not determine the extent. The east shore lay off to our right a half a mile or so distant, where we could see the miniature waves break on the beach, and at times, catch the sound as they rolled up on the gravel banks. We soon realized our danger, but feared to attempt a landing in the surf. Evidently the wind was increasing, the clouds were coming down lower and rain began to fall.

There was but one thing to do. We must make a landing, and so the sail was hastily taken down again, and the junior of the party took to the oars, while the senior sat in the stern with paddle in hand to keep the boat steady on her course, and help a little as opportunity offered. But fortune favored us in luckily finding a smooth pebbly beach, and while we got a good drenching in landing, and the boat partially filled before we could haul her up out of reach of the surf, yet we lost nothing outright, and suffered but slight loss by damage from water. We were glad enough to go ashore and thankful that the mishap was no worse. Luckily our matches were dry and a half hour or so sufficed to build a rousing camp fire, haul our boat above high tide, and utilize it as a wind break and roof turned bottom up at an angle of forty-five degrees. Just how long we were compelled to remain in this camp, I cannot recall, but certainly two days, and I think three, but we did not explore the adjacent land much, as the rain kept us close in camp. And it was a dismal camp, although we had plenty to eat and could keep dry and warm. We here practiced the lesson taught us the evening of our first camp, by the native matron, and had plenty of clams to supplement our other provisions during the whole period, and by the time we broke up camp, concluded we were expert clam-bakers. But all such incidents must have an end, and so the time came when we broke camp and pulled for the head of Whidby's Island, a few miles off to the northwest.

And now, I have a fish story to tell. I have always been shy of telling it, lest some smart one should up and say I was just telling a yarn and drawing on my imagination, but "honor bright," I am not. But to be sure of credence, I will print the following telegram recently received, which, as it is printed in a newspaper, must be true.

Nanaimo, B. C., Friday, Jan. 29.
Another tremendous destruction of herring occurred on the shores of Protection Island a day or two ago in exactly the same way as took place near Departure Bay about three weeks ago, and today the entire atmosphere of the city carries the nauseous smell of thousands upon thousands of tons of decaying fish which threatens an epidemic of sickness.

The dead fish now cover the shores of Protection Island continuously for three miles to a depth ranging all the way from fifteen inches to three feet. The air is black with sea gulls. So thick have the fish been at times that were a fishing boat caught in the channel while a shoal of herring was passing, the rush of fish would literally lift the boat out of the water.

We had not proceeded far before we heard a dull sound like that often heard from the tide-rips where the current meets and disturbs the waters as like in a boiling caldron. But as we approached the disturbance, we found it was different from anything we had seen or heard before. As we rested on our oars, we could see that the disturbance was moving up toward us, and that it extended as far as we could see in the direction we were going. The sound had increased and became as like the roar of a heavy rainfall, or hailstorm in water, and we became aware that it was a vast school of fish moving south while millions were seemingly dancing on the surface of the water and leaping in the air. We could sensibly feel them striking against the boat in such vast numbers as to fairly move it as we lay at ease. The leap in the air was so high as to suggest tipping the boat to catch some as they fell back, and sure enough, here and there one would leap into the boat. We soon discovered some Indians following the school, who quickly loaded their canoes by using the barbed pole as a paddle and throwing the impaled fish into their canoes in surprising numbers. We soon obtained all we wanted by an improvised net.

We were headed for Whidby's Island, where, it was reported, rich prairie land could be found. The bay here at the head of the island was six or seven miles wide and there was no way by which we could keep near shore. So far as we could see there was no end to the school ahead of us, the water, as far as the eye could reach, presenting the appearance shown with a heavy fall of hail. It did seem at times, as if the air was literally filled with fish, but we finally got rid of the moving mass, and reached the island shore in safety, only to become again weather bound in an uninhabited district of country that showed no signs of the handiwork of civilized man.

This camp did not prove so dreary as the last one, though more exposed to the swell of the big waters to the north, and sweep of the wind. To the north we had a view of thirty miles or more where the horizon and water blend, leaving one in doubt whether land was in sight or not, though as we afterwards ascertained, our vision could reach the famous San Juan Island, later the bone of contention between our government and Great Britain. Port Townsend lay some ten miles northerly from our camp, but was shut out from view by an intervening headland. Marrowstone Point lay about midway between the two, but we did not know the exact location of the town, or for that matter, of our own. We knew, like the lost hunters, where we were, but the trouble was, we "didn't know where any place else was." In front of us, the channel of Admiralty Inlet here but about four miles wide, stretched out to the north into a fathomless sea of waters that for aught we knew, opened into the wide ocean. Three ships passed us while at this camp, one, coming as it would seem from out of space, a mere speck, to a full fledged, deep sea vessel, with all sails set, scudding before the wind and passing up the channel past us on the way to the anchorage of the seven vessels, the other two gracefully bearing their way out against the stiff breeze to the open waters beyond. What prettier sight can one see than a full rigged vessel with all sails spread, either beating or sailing before the wind? We had, as a matter of prudence, canvassed the question of returning from this camp as soon as released from this stress of weather, to the bay of the anchored ships in the more southern waters, but the sight of these ships, and the sight of this expanse of waters, coupled with perhaps a spirit of adventure, prompted us to quietly bide our time and to go farther, when released.

It was a calm, beautiful day when we reached Port Townsend, after a three hours run from our camp on the island. As we rounded Marrowstone Point, near four miles distant, the new village came into view. A feeling of surprise came over us from the supposed magnitude of the new town. Distance lends enchantment, the old adage says, but in this case the nearer we approached the embryo city, the greater our admiration. The beautiful, pebbly beach in front, the clear, level spot adjoining, with the beautiful open and comparatively level plateau in the background, and with two or three vessels at anchor in the foreground, there seemed nothing lacking to complete the picture of a perfect city site. The contrast was so great between the ill-smelling lagoon of Seattle or the dismal extensive tide flats of Olympia that our spirits rose almost to a feeling of exultation, as the nose of our little craft grounded gently on the beach. Poor, innocent souls, we could not see beyond to discover that cities are not built upon pleasure grounds, and that there are causes beyond the ken of man to fathom the future destiny of the embryo towns of a new commonwealth.

Upon closer examination of the little town, we found our first impression from the distance illusory. Many shacks and camps, at first mistaken for the white men's houses, were found to be occupied by the natives, a drunken, rascally rabble, spending their gains from the sale of fish and oil, in a debauch that would last as long as their money was in hand.

This seemed to be a more stalwart race of Indians, stronger and more athletic, though strictly of the class known as fish Indians, but better developed than those to the south, from the buffeting received in the larger waters of the straits, and even out in the open sea in their fishing excursions with canoes, manned by thirty or more men.

The next incident of the trip that I can remember, is when we were pulling for dear life to make a landing in front of Colonel Ebey's cabin, on Whidby's Island, opposite Port Townsend. We were carried by the rapid current quite a way past the landing, in spite of our utmost efforts. It would be a serious thing to be unable to land, as we were now in the open waters, with a fifteen mile stretch of the Straits of Fuca before us. I can remember a warm greeting at the hands of Ebey, the first time I had ever seen him. He had a droll stoppage in his speech that at first acquaintance would incline one to mirth, but after a few moments conversation, such a feeling would disappear. Of all the men we had met on the whole trip, Colonel Ebey made the most lasting impression. Somehow, what he did say came with such evident sincerity and sympathy, and with such an unaffected manner, that we were drawn close to him at once. It was while living in these same cabins where we visited him, that four years later the northern Indians, from British Columbia, came and murdered him and carried off his head as a trophy of their savage warfare.

We spent two or three days in exploring the island, only to find all the prairie land occupied, but I will not undertake from memory to name the settlers we found there. Somehow, our minds went back to the seven ships we had seen at anchor in front of Steilacoom; to the sound of the timber camps; to the bustle and stir of the little, new village; to the water activities that we saw there than anywhere else on the waters of the Sound, and likewise my thoughts would go beyond to the little cabin on the Columbia River, and the little wife domiciled there, and the other little personage, and so when we bade Colonel Ebey good bye it was the signal to make our way as speedily as possible to the waters of the seven ships.

Three days sufficed to land us back in the coveted bay with no greater mishap than getting off our course into the mouth of Hood's Canal, and being lost another half day, but luckily going on the right course, the while.

I look back with amazement at the rash undertaking of that trip, so illy provided, and inexperienced, as we were, and wonder that we escaped with no more serious mishap than we had. Upon the whole, it was a most enjoyable trip, and one, barring the risk and physical inability to play my part, I could with great enjoyment encounter the same adventure of which I have only related a mere outline. Did you ever, reader, take a drive, we will say in a hired outfit, with a paid coach-man, and then take the lines in your own hands by way of contrast? If so, then you will realize the thrill of enjoyment where you pull your own oars, sail your own craft, cook your own dinner, and lie in your own bed of boughs, and go when and where you will with that keen relish incident to the independence and uncertainties of such a trip.

TWO

Massacre at Ganges
and
The Salt Whisky War

by Bruce McKelvie

Massacre at Ganges

Few who visit the peaceful places of Saltspring Island today can visualize that in earlier times settlers had to face danger and death to establish themselves on its shores. The Island was first known as Chouan; later it was officially named Admiral Island, but the custom of calling it after the saline springs at its northern end overcame all attempts to have it designated otherwise.

It was always an attractive place and it made appeal to men who had been drawn to the country by discovery of gold on the Fraser River. Settlement started at Ganges Harbor and near Fernwood Point on the Northeast side. These places were continually menaced by the savage armadas from the north, while the settlers had to be constantly on guard against the treachery of the rovers from the big Indian villages in the Cowichan Valley.

There were four of these villages, from which long canoes went out to search the seaways amongst the Gulf Islands and take what advantage they could of travellers. The warriors from Quamichan were especially notorious and many a lone white man vanished, and even small parties disappeared. The secret of their continued absence was known only to members of that tribe or to other Cowichan braves. They, too, had to be on the alert, for when the mighty Haidas from the Queen Charlotte Islands, or the haughty Kwakiutls from the labyrinth of waterways north of Comox came in their great dug-outs, they were in danger of being butchered. These fleets of savage Northmen skirted along the eastern shores of Saltspring by way of what is now Trincomali Channel (named after a warship, *Trincomalee*). They brought terror to the settlers, who dared not show resentment of their thieving. The white residents never knew the day nor the hour when primordial warfare would flame about them.

George Macaulay was a man of experience in dealing with the Indians, but he was disliked by the Cowichans who did not trust him, claiming that he had failed to pay a debt due to one of their chiefs. It may have been this dislike and distrust that was responsible for the terrible massacre of July 4, 1860, in Ganges Harbor, when eight Bella Bella Indians were killed by the Cowichans, for they were crew-men of Macaulay's canoe. Again, a killing of two Cowichans, several days earlier, by a party of Fort Rupert Indians from the north, may have been the cause. Indian vengeance did not require that retaliation be made upon the individuals responsible for hostile acts, but only the spilling of strangers' blood.

Some white settlers were fishing off the north end of the Island on the western side; near them were two Cowichans similarly engaged. Suddenly a fleet of Fort Rupert canoes rounded a point. The Cowichans abandoned their lines and paddled to the white men's boat into which they climbed for sanctuary. The Northerners did not hesitate, they too, came up to the boat, clambered aboard and killed the Cowichans, cutting off their heads. They did not molest the whites.

On the morning of July 4, Macaulay was on his way to Fort Victoria from Bella Bella. He had business to transact with some of the Saltspring Island settlers. When, however, he attempted to land at the northeast settlement where the cluster of buildings had gained the local name of "Beggsville", the Cowichans there made such a hostile demonstration against his crew that he abandoned the attempt and continued on to Ganges.

What happened is best told in the words of Macaulay himself, and he set them down in a deposition made a few days later: . . . "About 2 p.m. I landed from a canoe in which there were nine men, three women, and one boy, all of the Bella Bella tribe . . . On touching the shore I fancied there was a hostile spirit evinced by a large party of Cowichan Indians on the beach . . . I spoke to the Cowichans, telling them that the Bella Bellas were good Indians . . . and that I trusted that the Cowichans would treat them as friends . . . They, in answer, assured me that they had no intention of molesting the Bella Bellas."

Accepting the word of the treacherous Cowichans, whom he had reason to suspect, for they kept their blankets about them, as if concealing weapons, Macaulay took a chance and left his crew to the mercy of their ancient enemies. For this he was later blamed by Governor James Douglas. He went off to call on Thomas Lineker, a settler, who lived a short distance from the beach at the head of the harbor. He had scarcely reached the place when he heard outbursts of musketry. Turning towards the waterfront he could see the Cowichans firing at the Bella Bellas as they raced for their canoe, into which they tumbled and pushed off.

"It was evident to me," Macaulay went on, "that the Bella Bellas would be defeated, as the Cowichans numbered between fifty and sixty and opposed to them were only nine of the Bella Bellas.

"In about half an hour, three of the Bella Bellas having fallen, the canoe commenced retreating, upon which the Cowichans immediately manned their canoes and gave chase, a dropping fire being meanwhile kept up.

"The Bella Bellas threw overboard all the skins they had with them, in hopes that, to pick them up, their pursuers would lose ground, but the manoeuvre had not the desired effect, as there were a number of small canoes with boys in them, who were directed to secure the skins, whilst the Cowichans continued the chase, gaining on the Bella Bellas at every stroke of their paddles.

"As a last resort the latter made for the shore, intending to take to the bush, where they could avail themselves of the shelter afforded by trees &c., from the fire of their treacherous assailants. They succeeded in landing, and were received by another party of Cowichans who had lain in ambush at that place, expecting a movement of this kind on the part of the Bella Bellas. Being now entirely surrounded they were soon all killed with the exception of one man, who escaped into the wood, and two women and the boy, who were taken prisoners by the Cowichans."

Late that night, the wounded Bella Bella made his way to the home of Lineker, where the settler and Macaulay were keeping under cover. Lineker had sent his family across the Island. The night was being made hideous by the shouting, shooting and war-whoopings of the celebrating Cowichans. Quickly the wounds of the sole survivor of the canoe crew were bound. He had been shot through the cheek and in one arm. Then Lineker led him to the trail and instructed him how to reach the other end of the Island. What happened to him is not known.

Several days later, when the Cowichans had left the place, settlers gathered at the home of Lineker and requested him to notify the authorities. He wrote a letter to Governor Douglas. He told of the murder of the two Cowichans and of the massacre of the Bella Bellas, and asked for protection for the settlement.

Governor Douglas lost no time. He communicated with Admiral R. L. Baynes, who gave orders to Captain James C. Prevost, of H.M.S. *Satellite*, to investigate the affair. In his report to the admiral, Captain Prevost gave an interesting glimpse of conditions on the Island:

"The settlement on Admiral Island is divided into two distinct communities by a lake three miles in length; that on the N.E. side off which I first anchored, amounts to 25 souls. The other, at the head of Ganges Harbor numbers 26, extending over between five and six miles of wooded land. Some few houses have been built and a few acres of garden ground brought under cultivation. A trail connects one end of the settlement with the other by crossing the lake in a canoe. Each settler claims 200 acres, and as many of the lots have a quarter of a mile sea frontage forming one side of Trincomalee Channel, which the Northern Indians pass through on their way to and from Victoria you will at once perceive the defenceless state of these men. Their isolated position without any acknowledged head, no one to keep order, no one to organize them, has caused a feeling of anxiety among them."

There was not much that Prevost could do, for, after all, except for the things belonging to Macaulay in the canoe, no harm had been done to any white settler, and the authorities were in no position to punish natives for inter-tribal wars. The *Satellite*, however, steamed over to Cowichan Bay, and Captain Prevost went up the river to Quamichan. He assembled the chiefs and told them that such acts of barbarity must cease. The Indians floored him when they agreed not to make war on other tribes if the Government would guarantee that others would not attack them. The Cowichans readily surrendered a woman prisoner and restored Macaulay's property, as far as they could for some of it had been sent over to the Fraser River. Captain Prevost sent Lieutenant Roche across the Gulf in the warship's launch in an endeavor to gather more of the stolen property. Beyond that there was nothing to be done.

The Salt Whisky War

It was a bright, lazy morning in May 1861. The gentle, vagrant whiffs of wind scarcely ruffled the water; the sails of the little schooner *Laurel* flapped idly as she drifted with the current in Satellite Channel off the end of Saanich Peninsula. The captain and crew of the *Laurel* were not unduly disturbed when they saw coming towards them around a headland a great armada of long cedar canoes.

It was apparent, from the size and high prows of the great dugouts that the approaching fleet was that of the Skidegate branch of the Haida tribe from Queen Charlotte Islands. These fierce warriors from the north made periodic visits as far south as Puget Sound and of recent years had developed a habit of spending some time on each such excursion at Fort Victoria. This was anything but welcomed by the authorities. They were bold men and fierce fighters. Less powerful bands of Indians were frightened of them. Even the white men were not comfortable when some hundreds of their guests were camped on the edge of the town. There was always the danger of a collision, if not with the whites then with the local tribesmen.

The Haidas had been particularly annoying during their stay at Victoria that spring of 1861. While there had been no concerted defiance of the law, individual cases of pilfering had been many. Now, however, they were on their way home with canoes well filled with the proceeds of their stay.

The men on the *Laurel* were no more particular how they made profits than were the savage vikings from Queen Charlotte Islands. There was a keg of whisky hidden away on the schooner for just such a marketing opportunity. But of what use would one keg be to such a vast host, for the *Laurel's* captain, through his glass, could estimate that there were several hundred Indians in the cedar flotilla. He had an idea. There was an empty keg on board. Without a moment's hesitation it was secured; the container with its whisky was uncovered, and half of its contents was transferred to the empty keg and both were filled with sea water.

Chief Jefferson and several other head-men of the Haidas boarded the schooner. Did the captain have any whisky for sale? He did. He had two kegs of fire-water. A bargain was soon made. The Haidas resumed their voyage. Then it was decided that a halt should be made to test and taste the quality of the liquor.

The Indians turned. They raced back towards the schooner. The white men, frightened now, sought to work sweeps to aid their craft, for the breezes that came fitfully did not drive them far towards land. There was no escaping the wrathful Haidas who quickly surrounded and boarded the schooner. They did not inflict personal injury to the white men, wily old Jefferson keeping his braves in hand to that extent; but the chiefs and nobles went to work in a systematic manner. They stripped the *Laurel* of everything moveable. Then they angrily paddled off.

The Haidas were still mad when they rounded Saltspring Island and started up Trincomali Channel. The homes and store-houses of the pioneer settlement of Beggsville came in sight. It was probably a desire to replace the salted liquor with some that was more palatable that caused them to land. They raided the store-houses and looted them. Then, still without ardent spirits, they headed for Nanaimo. Here they stayed for a day or two and sold off some of their loot.

In the meantime the *Laurel*, empty of everything but an enraged crew, managed to reach Victoria, where bitter complaint was made to the authorities against the action of the Indians—but nothing was said of the little transaction that preceded the looting of the schooner.

Governor Douglas was indignant. Something drastic must be done; these Haidas must be taught to respect the white man's laws. He communicated with the naval authorities at Esquimalt. Rear Admiral Sir Thomas Maitland concurred with Governor Douglas; the natives must be taught a lesson. Lieutenant-Commander Charles R. Robson, captain of H.M.S. *Forward*, was ordered to proceed in pursuit of the Indians.

Just as the *Forward* was about to sail, a fast canoe sped into the harbor bringing news of the happenings at Beggsville. The courier told of how Edward Mallandaine's store-house had been raided and some property taken; then that of Begg—the original settler— was broken into and most of its contents taken. With this additional intelligence Captain Robson made all speed on the track of the Indians.

Now, let the story be continued by Captain Robson, as he related it to the Admiral: "... I was informed by Mr Begg of the depredations committed by a large party of Northern Indians, who stopped at the N. E. settlement on the 9th instant and in broad daylight broke into a store-house of his, carrying off flour, potatoes, turnips and a flag. While thus engaged in plundering, Mr Sampson, one of the settlers, hearing the noise ran down to the beach, but was warned off by the marauders threatening his life if he approached. Previous to this, they had broken into and quitted the house of Mr Mallandaine, another settler. The settlers I found much alarmed."

After obtaining first hand information from the Saltspring Island community Captain Robson followed in the wake of the war canoes. When he reached Nanaimo, the captain was given further lurid details of the wicked actions of the Haidas—some true, others magnified. Here he found some of the nautical instruments and furnishings of the *Laurel* that had been bartered to residents of

Nanaimo. This, he was convinced, established piracy upon the part of the Indians. He consulted Magistrate William H. Franklyn, who, as a former master mariner, had acquaintance with the law and lore of the sea. Magistrate Franklyn was sure that the plundering of the *Laurel* could be defined as nothing else. He called upon the captain to aid the civil power in apprehending the pirates.

Up to this time Captain Robson's instructions had been to investigate the reports made of Haida depredations; now, however, having been formally called upon to assist the authorities, it was a more serious matter. The *Forward* hurriedly took on coal; accommodation was arranged for the Magistrate and Adam Horne, an experienced Hudson's Bay Company officer, who was enlisted as interpreter, and Edwin Gough, a fearless coal miner who agreed to act as special constable, a position he filled about the little coal mining camp. Messrs. Begg and Sampson, from Saltspring, were also on board to identify the Indians, if they could.

The gunboat made all possible speed in pursuit of the raiders, who had several days start. At last the Haidas were sighted. They had encamped by a creek just north of Willow Point on the shore of Vancouver's Island, several miles south of Campbell River, and about two miles from Cape Mudge. They had selected a strong position, and had thrown up temporary fortifications of logs and stones, for they were in hostile country, and might be attacked by the Kwakiutls. It was 6 p.m., May 17, when the *Forward* came abreast of the place. It had been learned at Nanaimo that the Haidas numbered some 300 persons.

Continuing his narrative, Captain Robson said: "I sent Constable Gough and Mr Horne, both well known to them, and unarmed, on shore, with a message to say that the Magistrate of Nanaimo was on board, to enquire into the nature of certain robberies . . . and to desire the chief to come off. Failing to do so, they were to be informed, that they would be fired upon.

"The first part of the message they positively refused to obey, the second they treated with the utmost derision, saying they had their guns and could fight and were not afraid of a 'schooner like that'. They became greatly excited, flourishing their weapons, seized hold of Mr Horne, who was afraid at one time they intended to detain him as a prisoner. I then steamed close in, hailed through

Mr Horne, and warned them of the consequences of their refusal, which they only received by shouts and yells of defiance."

At last the two men on shore managed to get away from the Indians and back to the *Forward*. It was a narrow escape for them. The Haida warriors were ready to fight. They had never refused combat and they would not do so now. They held the white man's "canoe" in contempt. They numbered as many fighting men as did the warship.

"Finding all other means of no avail," the captain went on, "I fired a shot high over the encampment, which was instantly replied to by a volley of musketry direct at the ship, the balls whistling thro' the rigging close over our heads and striking the side. Of course, after this, I immediately opened fire, directing the guns to be laid for the canoes, which it was my object to destroy in preference to an indiscriminate slaughter, which might easily have been effected ..."

The shot and shell from the heavy guns shattered trees, splintered the heavy logs that the Haidas imagined would provide them protection, and made kindling of fine big war canoes. Such havoc had never been witnessed by the natives, and when Shasha, a chief, crumpled and fell with a gaping wound in his abdomen, and another leader was killed outright and others had been wounded, the Haidas were ready to sue for peace. From the shelter of the woods they maintained a hot but ineffective fire. Only one sailor was struck, suffering a flesh wound to one of his legs.

At last Chief Jefferson came off in a canoe, waving a white flag. He was followed by other leading Indians. Magistrate Franklyn instituted an inquiry, after which he placed Jefferson and four of his sub-chiefs under arrest. They were charged with piracy.

On arrival at Victoria the prisoners were lodged in jail, and there they remained for some weeks. In the meantime the police probed into the circumstances surrounding the attack on the schooner. When they discovered that the whisky had been salted their sympathies were aroused. The unofficial opinion was that any white man who would play such a trick, even on an Indian, deserved all that he got, so the charge of piracy upon complaint of the captain of the *Laurel* was dropped. Chief Jefferson and his fellows promised to be good in future and were liberated.

THREE

The Cruise of the *Mineola*

by a Landsman

Vancouver, B. C. July, 17th, 1907.

Two of us could not swim, we were mere passengers, the Skip, mate and engineer could all swim. I feel more comfortable therefore now that I have smuggled a stray life-preserver on board which I found lying around the club float. I have hidden it in one of the lockers.

A gasoline engine boat had never impressed me favorably, in fact I had always been possessed of a more or less wholesome dread of the things. This one seemed to be all right, however, and besides we were taking out on this trip a young fellow who knew all about gasoline engines. Anyone could tell he knew all about them—he handled this one so gingerly. The boat is 35 feet long with a cabin in front which is a wheel house during the day, but can be converted into a stateroom with one single and one double berth for the night. In the middle is a fine pantry and small cooking stove on one side, and a well finished toilet room on the other side, with an aisle between them. Behind this is the engine room with two single berths and lockers for tools, dishes, oilskins, etc. The doorway out of the cabin leads on to a very commodious deck with an awning over it. All kinds of provisions have been put on board, and the other passenger and myself have been sitting out on deck for the last half hour smoking and waiting for the Skip to start away.

I forgot to say that this is to be a ten days' cruise—my first experience of the kind. I was at first very much inclined to stay at home, but finally made up my mind that if I was going to die I might just as well go this way as any other, so I accepted the Skip's invitation and here I am.

Here comes the Skip, so I'll stop for the present.

10 p.m.—Well here we are tied up to the float at the Pilot Station, just east of Point Atkinson. The Skip's a crank. Nothing to eat yet, although good things are commencing to smell up now. When he got down to the float this afternoon, he raised ructions. The new charts and coast pilot hadn't been put aboard. I know what charts are, but I don't know yet what a coast pilot is, and I am afraid to ask. Then no fresh water and Skip wanted to know if we preferred salt to fresh. When you come to think of it, of course, you have to take fresh water to drink. We got away at six o'clock, rounded into the narrows, passed Prospect Point lighthouse at 6:30 p.m. Passed the tug *William Jolliffe* with *Robert Kerr* in tow at 6:45.

Skip "tells off watches." He and I are on the same "watch." I suppose I'll learn what this is, too. The mate and John P., the other passenger, are the other watch. The engineer is to be on duty all the time.

We tied up at eight p.m.

Thursday, July 18th.

After a fine meal last night, the Skip took us all into his confidence and taught us things of the sea. I showed him this log. He and the mate laughed so much that although I at first thought of destroying it I have decided to keep it. I sleep on the "starboard side for'd." The Skip sleeps on the "starboard side aft."

We were up at six o'clock, had breakfast and were away at seven. Skip says I must say bells—seven o'clock is six bells. A magnificent morning, the sun shining on the distant snow-capped peak of Vancouver Island, the broad Gulf between and the dark green slopes of Bowen Island in the foreground made a picture not to be erased from this landsman's mind. We headed up Howe Sound. Passed Manion's at 8:30. Passed tug with boom at nine. Passed Bowyer Island, a round green knob, and proceeded on up the Sound. Ahead the Sound narrows to about two miles in width. Mountains rise on either hand from the water's edge to where their snow-capped peaks can look down on us basking in the sun six thousand feet below. Anvil Island, so called by Captain George Vancouver on account of its resemblance to a blacksmith's anvil, when seen from seawards, is left on our port side and in front of us Mount Garibaldi rears his mighty head as if barring all further progress. Nine thousand, eight hundred feet high is this monarch of the coast range. By this time we have opened up Thornborough Channel to the west, and leaving the main channel of the Sound we run close in by Defiance Islands on the north shore where Mts. Ellesmere and Wrottlesley rise almost sheer above us to a height of five thousand, eight hundred feet. The southern shore of this channel is formed by Gambier Island, whose moderate height simply serves to emphasize the immensity and grandeur of these mighty and everlasting hills.

I have just been making myself comfortable with some cushions when I am suddenly awakened to the fact that I am part of the crew of a well-ordered yacht, for I am informed by the Skip that it is now my turn at the wheel. I had noticed the "watch" being relieved from time to time, but had not realized that I, too, was subject to the same discipline. So for the next two hours I, the man who but yesterday was mixed up in puny affairs of business, guided the packet down that wonderful channel all by myself. To feel her answer my slightest touch thrilled me and the spirit of the whole scene, the mountains, the deep silent waters of the channel, the clear brilliant sunlight and the cool green slopes of the hills all entered into my very being, until I forgot that there ever was any other existence than this or cared whether there would be any other. Then the door from the galley pushed open and the gleeful query put, "Hey, your watch is up, how about eating something." So ended my first "turn at the wheel."

Friday, July 19th.

We anchored yesterday afternoon about five o'clock at Gibson's Landing. I found out this morning that after passing Manion's, we had been travelling all day at half speed. Fresh milk, eggs and berries were obtained ashore, and this morning we started up the Gulf for Buccaneer Bay. There was quite a sea rolling in from the south on account of a S. E. wind, which blew last night. I did not feel well. Of course, I was not sea sick, and took my turn at the wheel; but I think I indulged too freely of the fresh eggs and berries this morning. Every time the packet would leap for half her length over the crest of a big wave and dive down into the next, I felt as though she were going to keep right on going down, but with a chug and a sough as she hit into it she would give a shrug of her powerful bows and throwing a smother of spray high over her, would leap for the crest of the next wave. The Skip's eyes were glistening with delight, his whole face beamed, and every now and then as we would go through a good one, an exclamation of pure joy would break from his lips. Every one else was apparently enjoying it to the full, and after a time even I lost remembrance of those berries and cream and began to imbibe a little of the glorious spirit of the occasion, and felt genuine regret when at four p. m. we ran into smooth water, under the lee of Thormanby Islands. At 4:30 we entered Buccaneer Bay, giving its eastern point a wide berth to escape the reef which extends for some distance to the north.

Saturday, July 20th.

I was awakened this morning by the pitter patter of the rain on the cabin top. The high wind from the S. E. of yesterday afternoon and evening, had brought it up, and it is now coming down steadily and persistently. We decided that as we were very snug at this anchorage, and were in no rush, that we would stay where we were to-day.

We all went ashore last evening and visited a number of Vancouver people camping here. This is a beautiful summer camping grounds, and will undoubtedly become very popular. The mate and John P. went out in the dinghy this morning and caught a very fine salmon, which we had for lunch, that is to say, we had the most of it. The Skip is a good cooker of salmon. John P. worked the gramaphone all morning, and we have been entertaining visitors from shore practically all day.

This evening we are to attend a doin's at Mrs. C_____'s camp, which promises well. Altogether we did wisely in staying over here to-day. We are all wise. Skip says so, so it must be so. Besides the barometer is going up slowly, which the Skip says means fine weather tomorrow sure.

Sunday, July 21st, 1907.

This morning broke bright and clear. Got under way at seven o'clock. Turning out around the north end of the islands, we head for the distant shores of Vancouver Island. Texada looms up on the north like a great giant basking in the morning sun with Lasqueti, his watch dog sleeping at his feet. A light summer breeze is springing up from the west, turning the pale shimmering waters to a deep deep blue. The boundary line of the blue approaches closer and closer until finally we run into it. For the first time I see the Skip's face show a little dissatisfaction.

"What's up Skip," said I.

"Nothing," but I waited in silence knowing that a confession was coming.

"This gasoline wagon is all right, but the old *Swan* for mine."

The *Swan* was a sailing yacht the Skip used to own. Being a landsman I could not understand him altogether, and so attributed his remarks to some happy bygone trip in the *Swan*, memories of which were awakened by the present combination of circumstances.

The routine on board is now well established. One of my specific duties is to see that the riding light is properly in place every night.

My turn at the wheel comes on from twelve noon to two. It is very hot. Am steering by compass S. E. Everyone lying around in the shade where available. This is certainly a glorious day. The chug chug of the engine used to bother me at first, but I forget about it now unless my attention is called to it.

Away to the northwest, Sabine Channel opens up between Lasqueti Island and Texada. Then Ballinac's Islands appear to the westward as we draw nearer to the Vancouver Island shore. Away far inland on the island the hills rise gradually higher and higher, their wooded slopes of darkest green, here and there spotted with a settler's clearing, finally culminating in ragged mountain tops, all simmering in the afternoon sun.

About three o'clock we passed some bare rocky islets on our port side, and could catch glimpses of Nanaimo in the distance. About four o'clock ("eight bells" says Skip) we turned into Nanaimo harbor past Protection Island, with its derricks and heaps of coal and slag, and dropped anchor just south of the steamboat dock in a little bight so perfectly protected as to be secure from any wind that might come up. We all got on shore clothes, which felt very awkward and uncomfortable, and went up town. I think from the way the people stared at us that we looked as awkward as we felt. The Skip treated us to dinner at the hotel, and after looking around the town, came back to the packet and turned in early. Skip says I am the most industrious logger he ever saw. He says I should get in barometer readings. I'll start this to-morrow.

Monday, July 22nd, 1907; bar. 30.12.
Bright and clear. Breeze westerly. Left Nanaimo eight a.m. Headed down Northumberland Channel. Got out charts as the coast pilot warns against false narrows. By watching the south shore very closely, we pick out Dodd's Narrows, a veritable hole in the wall, scarcely 100 feet in width. As the tide was rushing through very fiercely we decided to wait outside in the main channel for an hour. Finally headed for the place and got through all right. After the first hundred yards it opens up, but the tide currents are extraordinarily strong, and the greatest care must be observed. After passing the DeCourcey Islands on our port side, we passed close by the wreck of a big steel freighter in the mouth of Stuart Channel. The story goes that a Swede captain, disdaining the services of a pilot, attempted to bring her out from Chemainus himself, with this unfortunate ending. Passing Porlier Pass, we caught a glimpse of the broad, peaceful Gulf and almost wished we were taking the outside passage, but the unlimited variety, the never ending wonder and delight of the scenery of these islands through which we are now passing, more than compensates for the difference.

At noon we passed the western end of Active Pass, and following the route of the *Princess Victoria*, kept right on for Victoria. At four p. m. the *Princess* passed us. We cheered her and got a response.

Tuesday, July 23rd, 1907.
We anchored in Victoria harbor at 7:30 last evening. A number of members of the Victoria Yacht Club came aboard and a very pleasant evening was spent. We are to spend to-day in Victoria.

Wednesday, July 24th, 1907.
Took the packet around to Oak Bay and anchored there. Had a number of Victoria friends aboard, who enjoyed the little trip.

Thursday, July 25th; bar. 30.4.
Bright clear morning. Breeze light, westerly. Got under way at seven a. m. (six bells). Made our course up the centre of Haro Strait. There is a fascination about taking to the open stretches of water that is not present amongst the islands, however attractive they may be.

Rounding Turn Point, we headed east for the Succia Islands, which lie at the foot of the open waters of the Gulf of Georgia, and ran along the International Boundary line for some miles, with old Saturna to the north and San Juan with its covey of little islands nestling around its shores, to the south. As we passed the East Point lighthouse on the extreme southerly point of Saturna, we left behind us the sheltering protection of our home land for at this point we cross the boundary line into Uncle Sam's territory. Leaving Patos Island to the north, we skirted along the northern shores of the Succia's (Skip says, pronounce it Sushia). Towards the eastern point of these islands, they become much broken up and would make a bad lee shore in a gale. We rounded this eastermost point, giving it a wide berth on account of reefs, and turning to the west ran up into the prettiest little bay I have ever seen. Nothing is too good to say of Echo Bay. It is more like a dreamland than an actual living place. These little islands, in no place more than one hundred feet high, lie in the form of a horseshoe and Echo Bay is formed by the two arms. The islands are well wooded, but

34

with little underbrush, giving them the appearance of a well-kept park. We ran up to the head of the bay, and anchored about two hundred feet from the shore. Having made everything snug,we went ashore, landing on a smooth pebble beach. A remarkable thing was the absolute cleanliness of the place. The water was clear and sparkling, the pebbles on the beach were brilliant in their whiteness, even the driftwood seemed to be all scoured and cleaned for our reception. There were indications of deer, but as we wandered through the trees and across the neck to the western shore of the islands, we discovered that they were otherwise uninhabited. An old fence and a few old deserted shacks now in a tumbledown condition indicated, however, that at one time human beings dwelt on the islands living what must have been an ideal existence.

At ten o'clock to-night I went up on deck to inspect the riding light before turning in. The night was perfectly calm. The moon was full. Away to the eastward, past the entrance of the bay, over the silent stretches of the Gulf and beyond the mystic dark background of the mainland, ghost-like loomed Mount Baker; his mighty height of snow outlined clear in the moonlight, keeping silent watch over this fairyland of ours, the same now as when he welcomed the first of our race over a century ago, and as he had done for ages past, and as he will continue to do for ages to come. Around about us lay the islands, the clear spots and beaches thrown into relief by the dark shadows of the woods. The little ground swell coming in from the Gulf gently rocked *Mineola*, and passing on broke with a ripple on the beach, intensifying the silence of the night. Finally the moon sank in the west behind the trees, and I went below to turn in. It was two'clock.

Friday, July 26th, 1907.

I awoke this morning with the smell of fresh bacon and coffee in my nostrils and heard a big splash overboard. I turned out at once and joined the bunch in a swim three times around the packet. After breakfast, the "engineer" said he had about an hour's work to do on the engine before we could get away, so we had a general cleaning up.

We got away about ten o'clock. Day bright and clear, with light westerly breeze. Our course lay right up the middle of the Gulf somewhat west of north. We were now heading for home. Soon the Succia's began to look far off and East Point lighthouse beaming in the morning sun was soon little more than a white speck. I think I mentioned before the fascination of getting out in the open. There is nothing else like it. Skip is at the wheel. John P. and the mate are reading, the engineer is looking at that engine as I have seen some children behold a favorite puppy, so I am going to go below and have a sleep.

Saturday, July 27th, 1907.

There is very little more to add to this log. When I woke up yesterday, Point Grey was in sight. We ran into Pilot Cove and spent the night there, and this morning, after getting everything ship shape, came into Vancouver, and here we are at the Club anchorage at the end of what has been to me the most delightful and altogether happy experience I have ever had. The whole crew have voted and require me to put down that this has been the most pleasant trip taken up to date on *Mineola*.

A Great River North: I

Eighteen Feet to Alaska

by Sidney R. Sheldon

In the spring of 1909, while I was on the faculty of the University of Idaho, an assistant professor of mining engineering whom I'll call Chesley and George Stevens, a senior mining engineering student, persuaded me to undertake a trip to Alaska in a small boat. We hoped to get a boat in Seattle, but we wrote for catalogues and found Seattle prices entirely too high for our purses. Finally we ordered an eighteen-foot Mullins steel boat from Detroit. It was to be delivered in Seattle about the middle of June. In the meantime we prepared a series of charts covering the route from Seattle to Skagway.

When we got to Seattle we found our boat had not yet arrived, so we put in the time seeing the Alaska-Yukon-Pacific Exposition until we were notified that our boat was at the freight depot. We immediately had the boat taken to a boatbuilder's shop for some necessary alterations, the shop owner to direct the work and supply the tools while we did the actual labor.

We put in a mast and sails, added a heavy keel to make the smooth-bottomed boat satisfactory for sailing, and put on a canvas hood forward to protect the engine from waves and spray. We also bought a red and green light, a pump and a fog horn to comply with the marine laws. The original cost of the boat was a hundred and ten dollars. The freight charges were ninety dollars and the alterations and equipment about a hundred, so the total cost was three hundred dollars or a hundred apiece. We put in a week refitting and equipping the boat and trying it out on Elliott Bay, then made a run over to Bainbridge Island. Finally, on a beautiful day in late June, we started north.

There was just room enough for the three of us to sit on the thwart amidships. The front of the boat was taken up by the engine and the mast, and the stern was filled with blankets, tent, provisions and extra gasoline. By late afternoon, well up on Whidby Island, we made our first camp on the beach. We set up our tent and cooked our supper over an open fire, then had a big bonfire of driftwood and went to sleep on our bough beds.

We'd expected to make an early start in the morning, but we found the tide out and our boat on its side more than a hundred feet from the water. The three of us couldn't slide the heavy boat, so we made rollers of logs and rigged up a block and tackle with ropes. By noon, after much arduous labor, we had the boat down far enough to meet the incoming tide. We arrived in Port Townsend that evening, made camp on the beach outside of town, and in the morning started bravely for Victoria, forty miles across the Straits of Juan de Fuca.

We had gone ten miles or so when the wind came up and large waves began to dash over the bow of the boat. The spray hood shrank as soon as it got wet and left a two-inch rim around its edge through which the water poured. It was not long before the boat was half filled with water and the engine stopped. We ran up the sail, but a gust of wind broke the main boom about a foot from the mast. By this time Chesley had gone to pieces. He was crying, telling us goodby, saying he would never see his mother again, and making a general fool of himself.

In the meantime I got hold of the end of the boom and held it while I headed the boat with the wind and back toward Port Townsend. Stevens cussed Chesley out thoroughly and got him to bailing, then went to work on the engine. With the sail up, we stopped taking in water and Stevens got the engine started. We got back to Port Townsend without further mishap.

The next day we spent drying our equipment, having our boom reinforced, and sewing an extra four inches of canvas around the bottom of our spray hood so the water couldn't beat in. Chesley refused to try for Victoria again, so we went back around the lower end of Whidby Island and followed the sheltered passage through the San Juan Islands to Sidney on Vancouver Island. From Sidney we followed the protected waters of Saanich Inlet and Stuart Channel to Nanaimo. It was a most picturesque and delightful trip, with some of the most beautiful sea and island scenery I've ever seen.

Chesley evidently was not built for a seafaring life. He became increasingly nervous with the slightest bit of rough water. Just before we reached Nanaimo he told us he had been thinking about his sister, who was ill in Denver, and that if she died while he was gone he would never forgive himself. Therefore he had decided to take a steamer back from Nanaimo and go to see her.

We made camp on Gabriola Island opposite Nanaimo, then in the morning ran across to lay in a supply of provisions and gasoline and allow Chesley to arrange his passage back to Seattle. We all had lunch at a restaurant and Chesley ordered a round of drinks to the success of our voyage. Then Stevens insisted upon drinking to the health of Chesley's sister. Finally Stevens and I said goodby to Chesley and started back to camp.

When we arrived we found that one package of groceries had been left out of the boat. Stevens offered to run back to Nanaimo for the groceries while I cooked supper, and left saying he would be back by six o'clock. At eight I saw the boat coming back with two men, one of them standing. It seems Stevens had insisted that the clerk who had forgotten the groceries should have a drink with him to show there were no hard feelings. Then the clerk had to set up drinks to show he was sorry, and so on.

They had supper and then we had to take the clerk back. Then Stevens had to give the clerk a farewell drink and the clerk had to return it, and so on all over again. I kept trying to get Stevens away and he kept saying, "I'm as sober as a judge."

Back at the boat finally, he wanted to take the tiller but I wouldn't let him. Then he decided he would oil the engine, saying, "We're going to make a record run!" Each time he would lean forward to oil the engine he would topple forward and short-circuit the spark plug on the top of the engine. This would give him a violent shock and he would let out a yell. Finally he settled down and went to sleep.

When we reached shore I took the groceries and Stevens insisted upon anchoring the boat. We had landed on a point and it was necessary to walk around a small inlet to get to the tent. Stevens tried to walk across but ran into deep water. Then he tried farther up and fell down in the shallow water and mud and couldn't get up. Finally I hauled him out of his wallow, dragged him over to the camp, poured a couple of pails of water over him to wash off part of the mud, and rolled him up in his blanket. By this time it was nearly midnight.

We had agreed to be up at four a.m. so we could break camp, pack up and make a run over to Texada Island across Georgian Bay. Accordingly, but not without difficulty, I awakened Stevens at four and by seven o'clock we were on our way.

Along about eleven, when it was getting good and hot on the water, Stevens began to complain of a headache and hint that it was time to make camp, but I kept going until well along in the afternoon. We made camp in a beautiful little bay at the upper end of Texada Island and stayed there two or three days. We dug clams, paddled around in a kayak we found, and climbed the hill back of camp.

Then we continued northward without any noteworthy happenings until we ran into a storm up Johnstone Strait. The breakers were so bad on shore that we found it impossible to land, but finally we made a landing in the lee of an island. At least, we managed to get ashore with the mooring rope, though we hit a rock that tore a hole in the bottom of the boat, and it sank immediately. We spent the next two or three days drying out our equipment and repairing the boat, cutting up our baking pan to make a patch.

Well started on our way again, we discovered that our gallon can of lubricating oil had floated off when the boat had sunk. By being careful with what oil we had in our small can, we managed to get to the northern end of Vancouver Island, where we found a small trading post and bought two quarts of oil.

We now had eighty miles of Queen Charlotte Sound to cross, open to the Pacific with nothing to the west of us except China. To make an early start before the wind came up, we left at four in the morning of a beautiful, calm day. We'd have made it easily except that we began to have engine trouble, caused by the fact that we had been too thrifty with oil the preceding days.

Along in the afternoon, off Point Caution, we dismantled the engine and cleaned out the cylinder. By this time it was raining and the wind was coming up. Having to seek shelter, we turned back down the coast under sail and finally about nine o'clock found a little river. Rain was coming down in sheets and both sides of the river were swampy ground covered with a snarl of great, fallen trees. It didn't look like a promising place for a camp.

I left Stevens trying to anchor the boat in a sort of whirlpool where the bottom was so rocky that the anchor would not hold, while I hunted for a camp site. I followed along the trunks of fallen trees until I found a hummock of moss. I could push my arm up to the elbow into this moss and the hole would immediately fill with water, but by spreading a rubber blanket as a tent floor I was able to make a place to sleep.

Meanwhile I heard Stevens swearing at the boat and the anchor, so I went back to help him. My first throw of the anchor was a lucky one. It held. We had some difficulty building a fire in a swamp in pouring rain, and Stevens got a little discouraged. He said if we ever got out of this mess, he was ready to turn back. But at last we found dry wood inside a dead tree and built our fire in the hollow of a stump. Soon we had bacon and coffee cooking, and things looked a little better.

In the morning we started on, but shortly the spring in the timing device in the engine broke, and we ran intermittently with an improvised spring of rubber bands. Finally we shut down our engine and sailed for a couple of days, and one afternoon, in a cold, pouring rain, we reached a cannery in Rivers Inlet. Everything we had was wet, including our clothes and blankets.

We hung our clothes and blankets in the boiler room of the cannery and sat around in our BVD's while our clothes dried. In the meantime, some of the fishermen turned over an empty cabin to us and prepared a big supper of ham and eggs, which we enjoyed thoroughly. After supper, in my dried clothes and a fisherman's slicker to keep out the rain, I went down to the boat to get the engine cylinder and timer, which the men in the cannery shop had promised to repair for us.

The tide was out and our boat was four feet below the end of a ladder down the side of the pier. With the heavy cylinder in one hand, I stood on the deck of the boat and reached for the ladder. The bow wave of a passing tug caused the boat to roll and I went into the ice-cold water over my head. I didn't let go of the cylinder, but managed somehow to get it into another boat tied nearby and pull myself out. Then I had to spend more time in the boiler room to dry out.

We stayed Saturday and Sunday with the fishermen at Rivers Inlet. Stevens got drunk again, had a fight with a fisherman, and fell off the elevated sidewalk into the mud of the tide flat — to the great amusement of a crowd of Indian women who were looking on.

From Rivers Inlet we followed the inside channels to Prince Rupert, seeing some wonderful water and mountain scenery and spending much time enjoying the trip. That last day into Prince Rupert was a long one, as we were eager to reach port and spend the night in a hotel.

Actually, we did not make the harbor until nearly midnight. Our chart had been issued before there was a Prince Rupert, and we found the various lights and lighthouses rather confusing.

As we passed the mouth of the Skeena River we met a big river steamer coming out. She was blazing with lights, a beautiful sight, but we were right in her course and having engine trouble. She blew her whistle then went around us, the captain making sarcastic remarks in passing. We ran out of gasoline and had to refill in the dark, then followed the steamer into the harbor.

Our arrival in Prince Rupert created a sensation. We were told that ours was the smallest boat ever to make the trip up the Inside Passage, and that we "had our gall" to tackle Queen Charlotte Sound and Milbanke Sound in such a craft. A lot of people came down to see "the little boat that came up from Seattle."

After a few days in Prince Rupert we ran to Port Simpson, thirty-five miles away and just across Portland Canal from Alaska. We ran into a heavy gale and had quite an exciting passage, as the wind was almost too heavy for our sail and the sea was too rough for the engine without the sail to steady it. We found that our boat ran much more smoothly in a big sea on sail only, as the engine seemed to drive it into the waves. On this run to Port Simpson we were afraid the wind would tear away our rigging — in fact, the boom was whipped loose once — but somehow we made the passage without taking on any water.

Starting out for Ketchikan, we found the wind and sea too heavy for us. After taking in a few waves we turned back to Port Simpson and waited out the storm. This was an interesting place — the original Hudson's Bay Company post on the Pacific, and the original blockhouse was still there. There were about nine hundred and fifty Indians, all fairly well-to-do. Many of them had fine, big, three-story houses.

Three or four other small boats were also laid up in Port Simpson and we had a rather jolly crowd. Most of them were college men, representing Harvard, Lehigh, Michigan, Idaho, Wisconsin, Houghton and California. Young Rittenhouse of Philadelphia, many times a millionaire, was in Port Simpson looking over the ground for a proposed railroad to the head of Portland Canal. We found him to be a fine fellow.

One of the most interesting men was Captain Shrove, there with his yacht. He had once owned the *Indiana*, the ship on which I had traveled to Panama the year before. (He had sold the *Indiana* to the Pacific Steamship Company some years previously.) He entertained us with stories of his seafaring life. When he found that we lacked good charts for one or two short sections of our trip, he gave them to us.

Captain Shrove had brought his yacht into Port Simpson under sail, as he was having trouble with his engine and the repair men in

Alaska had not been able to diagnose it. We offered to look it over. Luckily we discovered the trouble, dismantled the engine, had repairs made at the shop and reassembled it. It worked perfectly.

The captain was so pleased he insisted upon setting up champagne in his cabin. Then he and I went ashore. Stevens must have had more champagne with the captain's wife, as I had to put him to bed later in the evening. In the morning I told Stevens I'd had enough, and I'd start back to Seattle the first time he took another drink. He promised to leave the stuff alone, and I believe he kept his word.

We tried again one morning to cross Portland Canal, but without success. Then someone told us the wind came up every day and we'd better try to make the trip at night. Therefore we spent another day getting our stuff dried out, and left at eight o'clock in the evening, with a light offshore breeze. We were able to use both sail and engine, and as the tide was with us we made wonderful time.

That led to our undoing. We underestimated our speed, missed a lighthouse in the fog that had come up, and ran past the entrance to Revillagigedo Channel. At two a.m. we found the wind becoming stronger, with breakers on our starboard when we should have been in quiet water. About this time our gasoline gave out and I had to crawl forward around the mast to fill the tank with a spare five gallons we carried. I was so cold I had difficulty using my hands, and the boat was bobbing about on the waves, which didn't make things easier.

We had to keep going, but at four a.m. we got our bearings and found we were on the seaward side of Duke Island. The sea was rough, but by eight o'clock we got around the island and started up a sheltered channel. We had now been at it steadily since four a.m. the day before — twenty-eight hours —and Stevens said he was all in. About ten o'clock, in smooth water at last, we tied up alongside a flat rock.

Stevens threw himself upon the rock and was instantly asleep. I was not sleepy but I was hungry, so I started a fire, cooked a combination breakfast and lunch, and awakened Stevens at twelve. Then we started up the east side of Annette Island.

By three o'clock, when we had reached the narrow-necked entrance to a little circular bay, our gasoline pipe began to leak into the boat. We made temporary repairs with adhesive tape, then ran into the bay and made camp in a deserted log cabin.

This was one of our prettiest camps. Across the bay was a beautiful little trout stream with a series of waterfalls, and behind the stream was a towering, snow-capped mountain. The stream looked so inviting we ran up it as far as we could in the boat, then followed it on foot for about a mile and came back with a dozen good-sized trout. We also filled our hats with blueberries.

After a big dinner of trout, bacon, blueberries, hot biscuits and coffee, we went to bed at six o'clock in the blazing sunlight and both slept until about ten the next morning. We stayed at this beautiful camp for four days, fished, climbed the mountain, read and rested.

The remainder of the trip to Skagway was mostly sight-seeing in the coastal Alaskan towns, with camping in between. We had some more engine trouble just before we reached Wrangell, but got a tow from a fishing boat. We had to run the boat ourselves, as the owner turned it over to us and logged five or six hours of sleep. He said he needed it badly as he'd been drunk the night before.

We sold our boat in Skagway. Stevens stayed in Juneau where he had run into friends, and I returned to Seattle on the *SS Cottage City*. I had a pleasant trip with a jolly crowd, and rather enjoyed taking it easy on shipboard after two strenuous months in a small boat.

Moving into the Stream: The Inside Passage

The Strait or Gulf of Georgia, that separates Vancouver Island from the mainland, although widening at times to forty miles, is for the most part like a broad river or lake, landlocked, walled by high mountain ranges on both sides, and choked at either end with groups of islands.

Eliza Scidmore

FOUR

Saga of the Pacific Salmon

by Negley Farson

Part One

For over a month in the autumn it rains steadily on Vancouver Island, while the fogs curl through the forest and the mists from the Pacific are swept in. This northland has a melancholy grandeur then. And it is then that you may witness the end of the salmon's fore-doomed life span. You see the final act of the tragedy. You may witness, if you have the luck to realise its drama, the beginning of the new life.

Down below the river pool lived a Scot who had pitted himself against inexorable Nature to "better the odds", as he phrased it, of the Pacific salmon's chance for life. He was the hatchery-man. But he was so much more than that, such a fanatic, such a high priest of his cult that wherever since I have been fishing the picture always comes back to me of him standing there on that fish trap in British Columbia, performing his almost mystic rites.

Great green purple rocked mountains; storm clouds pouring in from the Pacific; driving rain drenching the forests; forests of spruce, of cedar, of fir—thick as the hair on the back of a dog—a wind-twisted, crashing maelstrom. We could hear the thundering roar of the Robinson, sluicing down to the sea, its rapids milk-white, foaming, swift as a hydraulic jet. A wild day, even for British Columbia when the rains are on. We could hardly row against the swift river.

"Hell," said the hatchery man; "I don't think we'll make it!"

I couldn't talk. "Just one more stroke and then die!" I groaned to myself (I said the same thing for two miles at the Poughkeepsie boat races); and at last we entered the reach.

"McPherson," I said, when the spots had cleared from my eyes, "the salmon aren't worth it. Nothing is worth so much torture."

McPherson was lighting his pipe — upside down — defiant of rain. He bobbed his head at the pool. I looked over the side. And saw the Red Host.

Great, red, pale-eyed salmon stared up from its depths; an army passed, phantom-like, underneath. Weary with sores, they shot in from their fight with the stream, rested, and then silently took up their pilgrimage again. Thousands and thousands of salmon, up from the sea, to spawn and then die.

"Ghosts!"

"Aye," said McPherson, "they're ghosts, right enough. Come three weeks every one will be dead. Look at that buck! He's half-dead already."

I looked at the fish; diseased, distorted, miserable thing. It seemed hard to believe that only a month or so back he had flashed through the salt water like silver. Then had come the Urge; he had turned his nose towards fresh water—the stream he had been born in two years before. The scales had dropped off his back, to be replaced by soft spongy flesh; his jaws had become hooked, the teeth emerging, until like some savage red dog he entered the Straits of Juan de Fuca. Fasting, intent on his mission, he had escaped the weirs, wheels, and nets of the canners, fought the swollen flood of the river, leaped, twisted and mounted the falls, won past the spears of the Siwash.

"I have seen them," McPherson broke in on my thoughts, "a male and a female, comin' up stream, with a gang of Rainbows trailing their wake, like a wolf-pack hanging on to the flank. Aye, and

I've seen the old buck turn and chase them away from her."

"Guts!" McPherson grated the words. "Pound for pound, inch for inch, the salmon's the gamest thing in the world. And you say they're not worth it!"

Salmon, to me, had once been something that came in a tin. A hint to the grocer would land the thing on my table. But McPherson was telling me things.

"An' for what? In a few weeks every one will be dead. They'll raise a stink in the land. You'll see them clogging the bars; this water will fall and leave them in lines on the banks. Ducks will come in here in swarms and stuff themselves so full of dead, rotten fish that their own flesh will taste worse than poison. The mallards stuff themselves; they'll feed on nothing but eyes. Aye, and the bears make a bloody mess on the snows. Millions and millions of salmon get snuffed out like a candle."

"Why?" I asked meekly.

McPherson gave a snort: "Why! Now ask me another. Could I, or any other man tell you why Nature is the damn fool that she is? You and I wouldn't be sitting out here in this tub in this damned awful weather."

(All five species of the *Oncorhynchus*—the Pacific salmon—spawn but once and then die. Sockeye, Spring, and Dog Salmon have a four years' cycle of life; Cohoes and Humpbacks two years. In some cases, such as the Fraser River and the Nass, there is also a small run of Sockeyes, having a five year life-cycle.)

Coming up-lake in the hatchery launch, a condemned Japanese fisherman, McPherson had talked of his work, explaining the need for such effort. Between Nature and Man, he contended, the salmon is on the verge of extinction. Left an orphan at birth (could you call an egg that) a salmon egg has just one chance in a thousand of producing a fish that will eventually return to complete the tragic life-cycle of his existence, i.e., to propagate his species. One in a thousand! A bad chance, indeed. Hence the hatchery.

The hatchery betters the odds, gets the fish out of the egg, past the yolk-sac, the fry, and well into the fingerling stage . . . and then turns him loose. He is a bit of a lad then, able to take care of himself; and even a cutthroat trout will have to move, and think, fast to catch him. Thus spoke McPherson:

"Eggs! Give me the eggs, and enough retaining ponds — and I'll re-stock the ocean."

There are people who maintain that the hatcheries have not proved their worth, that all their work is but a drop in the bucket; but this hatchery man was so convinced by the evidence of his own eyes that he did not even answer my hints along this line. He stood there on the rim of the fish-trap, with a salmon clasped by the tail. His right elbow pinioned its head to his side. McPherson's trained hand slid along the Cohoe's stomach towards the vent. A stream of cornelian globules shot into the galvanised iron bucket, beautiful things, about the size of a currant. "She's a bonny fush," said McPherson. He spoke as if he were milking a prize Holstein.

"A marvellous fish. Let's have another."

I dipped the net into the box formed by the upright wooden slats of the trap, and chased a fish around until I caught it. "Buck", said McPherson, after the barest glance. The mittened left hand closed over the tail; the fifteen-pound fish swung and a quick flip of that well-trained elbow imprisoned the head. Again the nubbly, intelligent fingers slid towards the vent. A stream, fluid this time, quite milk-like, shot into the pail. He turned and directed it into another pail, full of those amber-red eggs. Then he flung the fish back into the swirling, discoloured stream, where, as far as I can make out, it swam off feeling quite cheery and bright.

Like a research worker in his laboratory, the Scot peered into the bucket, and gently let a soft flow of water seep in over the brim and across the fertilising eggs.

"Watch it now!" said McPherson.

I watched a miracle take place in the pail. A mist floated over the eggs, almost imperceptible, so fine was its fabric. It was the "changing of colour". Now each egg was distinct, wrapped in its own little robe of Creation. A white spot on each showed that Life was now there.

Some quickly turned a light coral in colour. These McPherson deftly extracted and cast from him. They were already dead. He went over his "babies".

By now I was feeling his fatherly interest. I went after the last fish in the trap. A queer pair, the two of us, the Scot and I in that mountain stream in British Columbia; and a queer fish, that in the trap. A thumping big buck, already far gone towards spawning; the hook nose and dog-teeth showing plainly. Some male salmon are so distorted this way, with the growth of reproductive organs inside them, that the jaws shut on each side of each other like shears. This fellow looked vicious. Also, the fish trap was but a rickety contraption. We faced each other. The pale, yellow-eyed salmon seemed to be eyeing me malevolently.

"Whush! man"—the landing net was snatched from my hand, and with one deft, practised dab McPherson ended the battle. In a trice the big fish was locked in his grip. McPherson leant over the pail again.

I like to remember him there, mist-wreaths curling about him, smoke-like, his red beard aflame. He might have been some High Priest conducting a rite, a Siwash *shaman*, perhaps, for the myths of the Haida Indians are peopled with salmon. The Haida had a belief that if a woman ate salmon eggs she would be turned into stone. High-prowed canoes, Siwash, McPherson, the salmon; they all belonged to this picture. The old Northwest that is passing. And McPherson, with his pails of red eggs, was fighting a rearguard action. Against . . .? Well, against Time, perhaps; Time and the Canners.

"A godless lot!" said McPherson of the canners, "with thought for naught but themselves."

Their money has made them a power in British Columbia politics. Strong enough to defeat (up to that time) any laws being made that would place a ban upon unlimited fishing. "Money," cursed McPherson, " 'tis all they are after. Catch all the fish they can—*and to hell with posterity!*" And the Future was the particular concern of McPherson. "Take care of those eggs!" He eyed me appraisingly before handing over the buckets. I stood there in the stream, the water pouring into my boots: "Take care of the eggs!" I retorted, "If you're not quick about passing them to me I'll pitch the whole lot in the drink." For an instant a fierce light blazed in the blue eyes above me. Panther hunters have seen it when in chase of the cub. I waded hurriedly off into the stream, the sacred buckets held high overhead.

McPherson, with magnificent assurance, ran along the 3"x 3" wall of the fish trap, and so got to shore. We made our way through dank undergrowth, dripping alders, devil's-club thorns, around the pillar-like trunks of gigantic spruce; and at last deposited the black-painted buckets safely on the floorboards of our rowboat. But the danger was not yet behind us; there was the river.

Great snags hurtled past us; gaunt, twisted branches, clawing arm-like at the air. A merganser came like a bullet up stream, making time—his red, wicked head stretched out like a spear-point. "Yon bloody bird!" blasphemed McPherson. "Every time he sticks his head under water—he comes up with a fish in his mouth."

We watched the sawbill shoot out of sight around a bend. "Here's hoping we don't hit one of those snags," said McPherson. It was like shooting-the-chutes at the White City. How a fish ever got up that current was a puzzle to me. We had only been able to get up the river by abandoning oars and pulling ourselves up by seizing the branches of the flooded banks. McPherson declared that a salmon could round a rock in a current running six hundred feet to the minute. It takes a seven-mile current, running steadily, to bar their continuous progress. "And they use their heads!" said McPherson. "They make use of every obstruction, sneak up in the back-waters and eddies—and then charge the swift water. Like *that!*" McPherson's fist shot past my nose to show the speed of their dash. It stunned you, the thought of this Homeric struggle, with Death as its final reward.

This yearly pilgrimage of the salmon made you wonder if, after all, there had not been some mistake made in the order of things. Fish like the *Tyee*, the Spring Salmon, which very often reaches a size of 100 lb., blotted out in their prime. It was too much like killing a man when he's forty.

We were now on the grey, sea-going launch and headed down the lake, where McPherson was going to drop me at my place. For the first time that day he relaxed. We had "stripped" thirteen fish. Three bucks and ten hen salmon. At 2,000 eggs to the Cohoe female, that meant ı that we had collected 20,000 potential salmon. Twenty fish would, by the estimated average, be all that Nature would have allowed to mature—twenty fish! But these eggs were now the protégés of McPherson.

They would be placed in long, wire, water-flowing troughs at the hatchery. In about 90 days queer little things would emerge. Fish about the size of a pin, with an odd little sac fastened to each. (The yolk-sac; its meals for four weeks.) When the sac would disappear the fish would be placed in retaining ponds and fed with grated ox-liver. They would live high on this and wax fat and strong. (I saw hatchery men, years afterwards, feeding ox-liver to the trout in a Somerset hatchery.) In about four months they would be about the size of one's finger—fingerlings. "But, this year," contended McPherson, "I'm going to keep them beyond that—say, six months or so. As long as I can. That will increase their chances. Every day adds. Then I can put them into the stream and not say, "God be with you", and think it's a joke."

But McPherson was, nevertheless, depressed. He claimed that the miscalculations of an engineer, over on the mainland, had, some years back, practically ruined the world's best run of salmon. And no man could put it back.

A few figures—"on the wrong side of the decimal point!" said McPherson—and a cliff face blew off that was not intended to blow off; it fell into the Fraser River, just when the "big run" was on; it blocked the river; and—"*Bang* went the world's best supply of tinned fish."

"What would you say," he asked, eyeing me for any dramatic reactions, "if I told ye that one push of a man's hand—the hand that touched off that dynamite blast—cost the Province of British Columbia, *and* the State of Washington, U. S.A, twenty-seven million dollars?"

"I would say you were balmy."

But McPherson, despite the gorgeous chance for histrionics in the grim tale he had to tell, was precise with his figures. Years afterwards, all over the world—being offered "Pink" salmon, instead of the Red Sockeye—I felt the brunt of this mathematician's blunder. Genuine Red salmon had become hard to get—even the price of the "Pink" had gone up; all of which you may find out easily for yourself when you try to buy salmon at any store in London today.

The reason for this world-catastrophe is another freak of Nature, in her seemingly reckless treatment of the salmon, known as the "Big Run" on the Fraser River. For some reason that has never yet been discovered there was a run of Sockeye salmon up the Fraser *every fourth year* that was always far bigger than the combined runs of the previous three years put together. This run occurred at precise intervals: 1909, 1913, etc., and would have continued—had it not been for this accident—again in 1917, 1921, 1925, and so on. This run was so big that even the most heartless fishing of the cannery companies, the traps and spearing of the Indians, the puny kills by sportsmen—nothing could even deplete it. Fish, massing into the Fraser on those Big Years, actually used to fight for space on the spawning beds. Nearly all the Sockeye in the world (the former commercial salmon) were hatched out on those beds. It is said that the three lean years—which even then were rich with salmon—could not aggregate to half the over-crowded "big year".

But when they were building the Canadian Northern Railway's tunnel at Yale in 1913, an engineer underestimated the strength of a blast he had ordered. Instead of breaking loose merely a calculated cubic quantity of rock, it knocked the entire face of the cliff into the river.

"It was a sight to make a man scream," said McPherson (who had been called over to help). "I watched thousands and thousands of salmon have a try at that leap. Men worked like beavers to help the fish past. We built fish-ladders on the side flumes; we hauled away boulders by sheer sweat alone. I tore the nails off me hands. We were frenzied, you know—we knew what it meant, if that Big Run did not get past. But it was no use. Millions and millions of fish died at the foot of the water shooting over those fallen rocks. They couldn't make it. Nine feet—the fish made the height—but they couldn't face a fire-hose. That's what it was like. Your heart broke when you saw that water hit them and hurl them back. With their eggs still inside them, they died—and with them died the Big Run of the Fraser."

McPherson declared that it was the most gigantic catastrophe known in the history of fishes. 1917—which should have been another "Big Year"—showed an 81 percent decrease of catch. It was certain that the Big Run could never be brought back. And for some years after the 1913 disaster the Canadian Government and the State of Washington could not agree upon a closed period for the Fraser. Too much money had been invested in the rival canning industries. Canners claimed that they could not stop—they must fish every year to cover their overheads. Interest must be paid, posterity notwithstanding, upon Capital. And, as the first twenty-five miles of the Fraser happens to run through American territory, there seemed no answer. Tit-bits of reform, eyewash for the Public, were achieved in making some of the poor Siwash Indians sell out their fishing rights.

In 1921—another "Big Year"—the catch was 93 percent less than that of 1913.

The Hon. William Sloane, Commissioner of Fisheries in British Columbia, declared: "Unless some radical steps are taken at once the salmon will soon be as extinct as the Dodo."

Years later (I do not know the exact date) an agreement of a sort was reached for a closed period to protect the runs on the Fraser. I do not know its result. It has not, from what I can see, yet made any effect on the market, and I write this as a purely personal affair—yours and mine. When your grocer offers you a tin of salmon with "PINK" on the label—whitish, queer-looking stuff, not at all like the firm, reddish flesh we were once so accustomed to seeing against the green salad and mayonnaise, you may think of this death of the "Big Year" on the Fraser.

For this pinkish stuff is not Sockeye. It is usually Dog Salmon, a fish that until the "Big Run" was destroyed was rejected by the canners—despised. Only fit for a Siwash! Humpbacks are now sold as "Pinks". By law, these names must be put on the labels. That is one bit of ethics which the Government have observed. The reason for the lack of colour in these fish is that the nature of their life-cycle is such that they are already advanced with their spawning process before they reach fresh or tidal waters where they can be caught by canners; reproduction has concentrated the colour-giving oil from their bodies into their eggs or milt.

They aren't bad. But I'd rather have catfish and waffles.

Part Two

One day, in British Columbia, you will wake up and find that the snow-flaked mountain opposite you has lost its flat, metallic colours of white, blue, and rock-grey. And the lake itself, instead of looking black as ink against the white snow marge, is a bowl of quivering blue haze. The sun feels unusually hot on your face. You can *smell* the forest behind you. Spring has come.

This was the real fishing! Spring, with the fly. I used practically the same flies I would use in Scotland, with the addition of the Cowichan Coachman, which has a plum and white wing, invented and tied by an English lady down on the coast. The seductive Alexander I found a dud in British Columbia, though I heard of other people having spectacular luck with it. Butcher, Zulu, the old reliable March Brown, Silver Doctor, Jock Scott, Grouse and Claret, Teal and Green, Teal and Red, with the exception of the Peter Ross (which I did not have there), these were the same flies you would use in Scotland, the Shetlands, or the Outer Isles. I nearly always used the Butcher for a tail fly, the Zulu for a dropper, and rang the changes with the intermediate fly. I used the same set-up in the Balkans, in the swift mountain streams of the Dinaric Alps with equal (if not better) success—plus the Peter Ross and particularly the hackle Blue Upright. I took the side-gangs off my spinning baits, finding I caught more fish by trusting solely to the tail gang. They didn't foul, hook so much, or near-hook. And I found a 2-inch, gold and silver, flat "Reflex" Devon —with one scarlet bead at its tail above the treble hook— outstandingly the best artificial lure. Again I emphasise the deadly attraction of that red or scarlet.

I had secured my house-boat then, this unpainted board shack built on a long raft of cedar logs; and in the lonely neck below Bald Mountain, where I moored it the next spring, I could always see the trout swimming about us in the calm of the early morning. I'll confess that in the very early spring I caught them with night-lines, baited with the illegal salmon eggs; but that was before they would take the fly. One had to live! I have caught them from our raft; but usually I left them alone in my vicinity. There was one big buck trout who *lived* under our raft. We used to watch him coming out— he used it for shade on the very hot days—and we could see him investigating the various bits of food we threw over to tempt him. We often debated whether he knew he was safe or not.

The partner of the Englishman who lived across the lake had come from tea-planting in Ceylon, found that the "ranch" in British Columbia was not the paradise he had expected when he sank his money in it, and he was soured. About the only thing that interested him now was fishing. He rowed across to me one dawn with the remark that he heard the Rainbow had started to take the fly "like anything!" in the river down below. What about it?

I don't know which is the most exciting; the thud when a fish takes the wet fly under the water, the "sup" as some big fish will turn and take a dry fly down—just before you hit him—or the last moments when you are, anxiously, about to land him. All of them of course surpass anything that a spinning bait can give you. There is nothing like the fly, or the pleasure of casting it.

On this swift river a line of logs had been laid along the other bank, linked by short sections of chain, to shunt off down-coming drift wood, brush, logs or whatever came down from the lake, so as to keep the river open. These early trout seemed to be lying always along those logs. It was not an easy cast owing to the high brush behind you, but when it fell and you saw your line sweeping down you knew that at any second the strike might come. A two-pounder would be a good fish in that swift water—too much if he took to the white water right away. Our bags were never very large, perhaps ten each in a day. A 2 1/2-pound fish was the biggest I remember getting there. But with a fresh spring wind blowing around you and that joy of being just alive, which comes after the long winter, every day was exhilarating.

There was a pool below where the house-boaters, and those who lived near the store, had a miraculous rise on some evenings. I have fished it with three or four boats on it, with fish rising all around us.

The back-drop of all this was the heavy fir forest, with the mountains above the timber line shining in the sun high above. The Cutthroat ran larger, but did not seem to have the same drive that animated the fine fighting Rainbow. Nor were they so good to eat. And by far the most memorable fish to me from those two years were two 2 1/2-lb. Rainbow, alike to the ounce, that I caught within half an hour of each other in my own bay. Both of them put up such a battle that I thought they must be four pounds at least. We were so sure of a fish when we wanted one that one night when we had invited the old Irish doctor over to dinner I didn't go out until the very last minute. The consequence was that I did not get a rise. Darkness had come down. I saw the long oblong of light from the open door of our house-boat, even heard the doctor's voice, sarcastically inquiring had I gone down to *buy* a fish from the hatchery—when a big brute, about three pounds, took my fly while it was sinking to the bottom.

Several times in the darkness he got under my boat without my knowing it, until I heard his fins and tail fluttering as he jumped behind me on the other side. My wife and the doctor, too, could hear the splashes; and he called—"Is that our dinner?" I called back that I thought it was. Then, with the fish in the boat, I yelled back triumphantly: "All right, Eve—put on the frying-pan."

Fish were no treat to the doctor; he was tired of them. But even his weary palate woke up when he had that one in crisp fillets, with *sauce mayonnaise*. Though he said grudgingly: "Seems an unholy waste of good mayonnaise." The fact was that the people who lived in those parts simply did not like fish. And as for salmon, they preferred it from a tin. I felt slightly that way about the British Columbia salmon myself, for it has nothing like the taste of a Scotch fish—no, it doesn't come within at least three thousand miles of it!—which is the distance across Canada.

But that spring I had so much work to do that an hour or so's fishing at sunset was an anticipated relaxation. I was working hard a good part of each day staining wood, making furniture, getting our house-boat in order. Then when the lake began slowly to fall as the melting snows vanished I marooned big logs on shore by wedging rocks under them, which logs, when the water fell, I thereupon began to cut up for our summer and winter firewood. The old German helped with a long two-handed saw to cut sections, and I helped him; then we each split up our own kindling wood. The sawing was a back-breaking job, for that German was a very tough and stubborn man, whose pride would not let him suggest taking a minute's breathing spell unless he was dead sure that I was ready for it. My flannel shirt dripped with sweat. Then, after a quick, naked dip into the lake, some fresh dry slacks and a clean shirt . . . the hour or so that I would idly fish along the shore was a luxury. These fish cleaned and lazily eaten, I would sit out in a camp chair on our "deck" and watch the stars come out. It is not an easy philosophy to trap with mere words—the feeling is not even tangible to yourself—but there was a peculiar "justification" in nights such as this which only "settlers" can feel. They will know, who read these pages. Then I would go to bed and contentedly read myself to sleep by the soft light of the old-fashioned oil lamp between our two cots. I read more good books out in British Columbia, and got more out of them, than I have anywhere since. In the morning, very often with the dawn, I would wake up with mind and muscles rested, take a dip overside after I had got the fire going and put on the coffee; or, if my wife was still sleeping soundly (which she seemed able to do until broad daylight), I would try a few casts before breakfast. Frankly, I preferred a good dish of bacon and eggs, with a slab of fried bread, to fish for breakfast; and we ordered our eggs from the Hudson's Bay Co. by the gross.

It was a delectable life. There were no mosquitoes to contend with, no pests, no neighbours (unless we wanted them), we owed no one in the world any money; I cannot imagine why we ever left it. I now put in several hours every day in hard writing, and had reached that point in the short-story technique where I was fairly certain that when I finished a story I would sell it. If I ever managed to finish it—which was quite another thing. But this certainty of having my stuff bought was the switch-over from the amateur to the professional attitude toward my work. It gave me satisfaction, security, and almost a ravenous interest in the use of words. The day when I realised I was checking and guiding the emotional impulse by a conscious control of form and words—was the day I ceased being frightened of having "no visible means of support".

From then on British Columbia could have been a paradise for us. We knew we could have lived there until we died. We had already been in communication with Alaska to get a small boat, with a sail, in which we intended that summer to cruise around Glacier Bay, but when that next looked-for spring came along, and we had already got so far as selecting the kit which we would take with us up to Alaska, I suddenly saw that if we did that trip we would be in

British Columbia forever. And there was a lot of the world I still wanted to see.

So we talked this over. My wife wept. She, of all the people I have ever known, was eminently suited for this life in British Columbia. She was self-sufficient both physically and mentally. She loved this lake, she loved the woods, she loved the absolute freedom of our existence. But she, too, thought that we should not "quit", retire in British Columbia, just yet. So she reluctantly agreed.

It was a sad night, that night—with the first of the up-coming salmon splashing as they jumped in the moonlight by our house-boat. The next morning I went down to have one last try for a big steelhead. They were running now, the river packed with 10-lb. fish. But although I fished over them all day, trying every way in the book, not one of them would look at it.

"Don't that beat the very devil!" shouted a man across the river, who declared he had come all the way up from Seattle just to fish this spring steelhead run. "I'm a-going to just take my damn rod apart and go home!"

I told him I was going to do the same thing. The next week we were on a train crossing the Rockies, bound for Chicago. I was going back to make money, all the money I could. This time it was going to be for a bigger jump. It was. Two years later I threw up the best-paying and most promising job I will ever have, sailed for England, bought a 26-foot Norfolk Broads yawl and sailed from the North to the Black Sea. But—

If I had caught one big steelhead that spring morning in British Columbia, both of us would be there now.

FIVE

An Island Eden

by Lukin Johnston

Two thousand feet below us, spread out like a moving panorama set in a sparkling sea of deepest blue, lay that wondrously beautiful archipelago known to the people of the Pacific Coast as "The Gulf Islands." As we flew southwest across the Gulf of Georgia from Vancouver towards Victoria, new attractions in these lovely islands were discovered every minute. In a hundred exquisite little rock-girt harbours, peaceful settlements were seen, trim white houses standing out from the dark forest background.

Many times on steamer journeys across the Gulf I had been charmed by the picturesqueness of these delectable islands. It is recorded that the Prince of Wales has said of the five-hour steamer journey from Vancouver to Victoria that "it is the most beautiful trip of the kind in the world." Thousands of visitors to the Pacific Coast will be ready to confirm H.R.H.'s opinion. But of the trip by air was born the determination to explore them more thoroughly and to learn something of the people who have chosen to live in these rocky little kingdoms.

So one day, when the sun shone bright and turned all the gulf waters into a shimmering sheet of liquid silver, I set forth to "discover" this strange kingdom.

We had been steaming southward from Vancouver for three hours. The siren hooted loud and long as we drew near the entrance to Active Pass. The old lighthouse at Georgina Point, which guards rocky Point Comfort, lay just to the south of the narrow channel —so close it seemed one could almost throw a biscuit to it. Gossip Island, a tiny strip of rock-girt land whose dark forested slopes looked cool and inviting, lay a little way to the north. A few hundred yards farther on, as the vessel swung round a curve, on the left there came into view, nestling in the shelter of a wide, deep bay, the chief settlement of Mayne Island. For no particular reason, save, perhaps, that it seemed to be a central point, I had chosen Mayne Island as the starting point of my pilgrimage. So at the wharf I disembarked from the little steamer —and proceeded to ask innumerable questions of all and sundry.

In the ten days that followed I wandered from one lovely island to another, walked for many happy miles through leafy country lanes, well gravelled, winding up and down dale, through thick forests of mighty fir and again out into the sunlight through fields where sheep and cattle browsed. At every turn I was reminded of some rural scene in Devon or Kent.

There are, in the aggregate, many miles of good roads on these islands which seem so small and insignificant to the casual traveller. Salt Spring Island, largest of the group, boasts 125 miles of fine automobile highways and by them you can reach all of the ten lakes on the island, in all of which there is good fishing. Mayne Island has seventeen miles of road; Galiano has forty. The latter, by the way, had no automobile until three or four years ago and some of the old-timers would like to go back to those blissful days, but to-day there are six cars on Galiano.

Under ordinary circumstances, if one's living had to be made without much capital as a farmer or trader, probably the choice of residence would not fall on the lovely islands in the Gulf of Georgia. But, fortunately, there are plenty of people whose circumstances are not quite "ordinary." Fortunate it is also that there are in British Columbia a number of people of modest private income who are able to seek out and settle in such a miniature paradise as this.

Probably nowhere else in all Canada within a similar area are so many unusual and interesting characters to be found. Ninety per cent of them are of Old Country birth, and almost all have private means. In my peregrination, to mention only a few at random, I met a remarkable old naval officer of over eighty who at one time served as first lieutenant on Queen Victoria's royal yacht; an ex-captain of the Royal Navy who first entered Esquimalt Harbour as a midshipman on H.M.S. *Phoebe* in 1870; a much bewhiskered, horny-handed son of toil who gravely informed me that until nine years ago he was a mathematical master at Eton, and a former Royal North West Mounted Police officer whose stories of thirty-four years in the force, chiefly in the north, kept me enthralled for a whole evening.

These people are by no means mentally deranged, though their tastes may differ from the ordinary run of mankind. It is a tribute to the climate of the islands and to the peaceful environment that you find here an amazing number of men, hale and hearty, who have passed long ago the allotted span of three score years and ten. It is true also that in few places in the world can the actual necessities of life be so easily wrested from nature. The soil is extraordinarily fertile; the climate is delightful; on most of them there is a fair supply of water from springs or wells, but the rainfall is surprisingly low, which is a drawback to farmers in some districts. The southern Gulf Islands have a rainfall of less than thirty inches a year, compared with fifty-seven inches in Vancouver and thirty-five in Victoria. As a compensation they average two thousand hours of bright sunshine every year, with an average summer temperature of sixty-two and a winter temperature of forty-two degrees. The waters abound in fish—ling, cod, herring and salmon of several varieties up to forty-five pounds in the sea, with trout and bass in the lakes and streams.

Before I undertook this expedition I should have laughed at the idea of a walking-tour on the Gulf Islands. They look pretty small when you pass them in the Victoria steamers. But on my first day on Mayne Island, for instance, I walked more than a dozen miles. But to begin at the beginning:

Mrs. Naylor, whose father was one of the first settlers on Mayne sixty years ago, fixed me up with a comfortable room. The window looked out on an orchard and there came to me the sweet perfume of wallflowers and the cheerful sound of clucking hens. Mrs. Naylor showed me over the hotel, lately enlarged to meet the needs of growing trade, and told me something of the history of the island. Mr. Naylor, by the way, was born in Victoria in 1865 and in the parlour of the hotel I spotted a group-picture of the Victoria baseball nine of 1888. In it appears the stalwart form of "mine host" as first baseman.

I started out along the road south from Naylor's, up the hills past McNeill's store and a number of small clearings. Presently, with a crunch of wheel and a rattle of harness and nuts, an ancient buggy passed me! Silly thing to record, I suppose, but it struck me as being quaint to meet a buggy nowadays.

A few minutes' walking along the hilly, twisting lane, past little clearings and substantial farms—the woods all fresh and green, and everywhere the subtle odour of burning wood—and the charm of these lovely islands was full upon me. I had been told (by those who did not know) that the inhabitants hereabouts were often a little "queer"—for the reason, I suppose, that they choose to live the simple life far removed from jazz orchestras, the roar of street cars and the constant danger of swift death from some erratic motorist. When I came to a white farm gate, leading down to a barn with a comfortable old farmhouse set in an orchard full of sweet-scented blossoms, I decided to "check over" this inhabitant at least.

And so I introduced myself to William Deakin, whose father settled on this place more than forty years ago. This farm, incidentally, has an interesting little bit of romance attached to it. It was taken up originally by an Australian named Nicholson, and even to-day the legend persists—if it be a legend only—that he had buried about the place considerable quantities of gold coins. It is said that, despite his reticence about any wealth he may have had, he used to turn up periodically and pay his bills in golden sovereigns. The theory came to be accepted that he had "caches" buried on his farm. Gold-hunting on the Nicholson place, at one time, was a pastime of Mayne Islanders.

From "Billy" Deakin, if I may become so familiar on so slight an acquaintance, I learned a bit of Canadian history. His grandfather, a retired officer in the British Army, came to County Simcoe, Ont., and took up an officer's land grant of two hundred acres near the town of Barrie, not long after the Battle of Waterloo. I gathered that many new settlers of that day went on the land under similar circumstances. The father of Billy Deakin, and of his brother Dalton, whose splendid farm at Village Bay is one of the show places on Mayne, came west by way of Chicago, Council Bluff and San Francisco in the 'seventies, and ultimately settled on this island. One could only ponder with admiration on the energy and courage of these pioneers who carved this fine farm from the thick forest.

Two miles farther on, all the way through leafy lanes or stretches of cool forest, I came to what is known as Bennett's Bay—for the reason that the three brothers Bennett have their homes close together. At the head of this sheltered bay, with the long promontory of Edith Point protecting it from the open waters of the gulf, there is a derelict hotel. It is no new discovery of mine that these islands will some day be regarded as one of British Columbia's chief playgrounds, for this hotel was built in pre-war days but never occupied, and only the coming of the war itself spoiled its chances of becoming a Mecca for holiday seekers. There it stands in dejected solitude, with green pastures all around it, a monument to someone's shattered dreams.

Dave Bennett, ploughing in the field, directed me through his brother Jim's farm, and so by a trail through the bush to Fisherman's Bay, a lovely spot at the end of a little valley. The sun shone bright and it was warm work trudging up the hill towards the point, so when I came on an elderly man in overalls leisurely clearing land and "stoking" the burning logs, I gave him "Good day" and asked if I might rest and smoke my pipe with him a while. We chatted about one thing and the other, and then I said:

"And how long have you been here, may I ask?" to which he made a reply that astonished me.

"Well," he said, "if you mean how long have I been living here, the answer is 'since 1912' but if you mean 'When did I first come to British Columbia?'—why then the answer is that I came to

Esquimalt Harbour first as a midshipman in 1870 on H.M.S. *Phoebe* under Admiral Hornby. Six ships of the line were in the squadron then—and that's a long time ago!"

I could not help but make a rough calculation of my new-found friend's age, and was the more astonished when he told me that when war broke out in 1914 he went at once to London and offered himself to the Admiralty for service. Somewhat hesitatingly, considering his age, he was offered command of a "Q" boat, which he promptly accepted and, in command of a converted and disguised liner, he was dispatched to the Mediterranean. Later Captain Henderson, for this, I learned, was his name, served with the Admiralty technical branch dealing with paravanes and other protective devices against submarines.

I took a different road back to Mrs. Naylor's hotel and on the way I called on the "Daddy of Mayne Island," in the person of Fred Robson, still active and running his farm, despite his eighty years. This fine old citizen came out from Pimlico, London, in 1863, and made his way to the Cariboo goldfields. A few months there—and he was broke on the coast. Then he heard talk of a railway coming through the mountains and so settled at Sumas. There he was flooded out and fifty-five years ago, in 1873, he came to Mayne Island. Of all the old-timers of that day—Murchison, Bailey and the others—he only is left, feeling the weight of his years a little, perhaps, but still in love with the island, where he has made his home for more than half a century.

I had covered about eight miles, but I was anxious to walk out to Point Comfort before nightfall, as the weather looked doubtful and I might not be able to do it in the morning. So I walked the three miles—a trifle weary, but well rewarded for my trouble.

As you enter Active Pass you notice the Georgina Point Lighthouse, on the south side of the pass. Just behind the Lighthouse is a large rambling building. It was built a good many years ago by poor Warburton Pike, the well-known big-game hunter, as a hotel. Some years ago it was purchased by Colonel and Lady Constance Fawkes. Colonel Fawkes, despite his threescore years and ten, has more than a local reputation as a water-colour artist, and in several houses I have seen fine samples of his work. I called on him and he, with the eye of an artist, insisted that I walk with him out to the lighthouse and see the marvellous view from there as the sun was setting.

We took our map, and Colonel Fawkes, lying on the ground, "set" it, so that we could locate Point Roberts, Steveston, the Lions and other Vancouver landmarks clearly. From Georgina Point you can look due north to Vancouver, and the whole horizon of splendid snow-capped peaks is like the teeth of a jagged saw. The glow of the setting sun tipped the peaks with delicate shades of pink and mauve, streaking the glassy water of the Gulf with faintest, ever-changing tones of blue, gold and red—such a picture as it was worth a few miles' walk to see.

I hurried back in the twilight through the woods, for I had promised myself the pleasure of paying an evening call on the doctor at the Mayne Island settlement. Eight-thirty found me at Dr. Christopher West's, and in him and his wife I found not only a very charming host and hostess, but an intensely interesting couple, whose reminiscences of the far North-west Territories would make fascinating reading. "Doc" West was for thirty-four years a mounted policeman, not as a doctor, though he held his medical degrees at that time, but as an officer for many years in charge of an area as big as an empire. At one time Peace River Crossing was his headquarters, and many a stirring frontier tale he can relate.

In a little shingled bungalow near the settlement lives Commander Eustace Maude, whose exploit a year or two ago in starting to sail to England by way of Panama in a tiny boat aroused world-wide interest. Commander Maude is in his eighty-first year. He stands well over six feet in his socks, and the brightness of his eye and keenness of his mind belie his silvery hair and beard. He is not through yet with the idea of sailing to England, and says he may try it again later.

At one time, many years ago, this fine old sea-dog was first lieutenant on the royal yacht *Victoria and Albert*. He joined the Royal Navy in 1861. After his retirement from the navy he came to British Columbia, his first effort being a general store at Duncan on Vancouver Island. He admits he was not cut out for that kind of a business and, selling out, he bought a sloop and cruised the whole east coast of Vancouver Island looking for the ideal place to settle—the essential point being that he must be on the sea and preferably where he could see great ships go by. They tell a story that on his first arrival at Mayne, he entered Active Pass in his sloop with sails set. He himself steered while Mrs. Maude pulled an oar on one side and a Chinaman on the other. At all events, there seems to be no more contented settler on the islands than Commander Maude.

In pouring rain Captain Denroche rowed me across to his kingdom of Gossip Island, but we went by way of Galiano so as to pay some calls there. We landed at Burrill's store, just inside the entrance to Active Pass, and here, high up above the water, so that it cannot be seen from the passing steamers, we came on a perfect gem of a rock garden. There is a little sloping lawn in front of the house, and to one side these two bachelor brothers have built up a perfect miniature Alpine garden—with scores of varieties of plants, a tiny artificial waterfall and graceful trees and shrubs as a background.

Lunch time found us at Whalers' Bay, where Mr. Miller Higgs is developing one of the unique places on the islands. Our host showed us round his "estate," which in years to come should be one of unrivalled beauty. He has taken in hand several acres of forest, and after clearing all the underbrush, will seed it to grass and plant daffodils and bluebells galore, making a lovely woodland park. Miller Higgs raises foxes, coons and rabbits and has them all scientifically housed. Foxes, as you probably know, require very delicate handling, and the roadway leading to their pens is barred to the casual visitor, so as not to disturb them.

The house, a picturesque bungalow set among fir and pine, contains many treasures which one hardly expects to find in such an out-of-the-way corner. For instance, the bedrooms have great four-poster canopied beds; there is a cedar-panelled billiard-room adorned with oil-paintings and bric-a-brac from overseas. There are old prints, valuable china and carved furniture not of our generation. On the rocks outside the house, the Union Jack waves proudly from a tall white flagstaff.

We rowed from this delightful spot to the farm of Mr. A. E. Scoones, who is generally regarded as an energetic and public-spirited citizen. He is the ex-mathematical master from Eton, whom I mentioned previously. He has been farming here for seven years. When I asked whether he preferred life on Galiano to that in England he replied, "Six months in England, nowadays, would bore me to death, I think." He stands something over six feet in height, and with overalls, bushy beard and hoe in hand, it was hard to picture him in cap and gown instructing the youth of England in the rudiments of geometry! I ventured to suggest that I should like to send a snapshot of him masquerading as a horny-handed son of toil to some of his erstwhile charges!

There is a fine community hall and a school, both of which we inspected on our way up the five-mile valley which runs due east and west on Galiano.

Late in the afternoon, after a strenuous but interesting day, we came to a haven of rest on tiny Gossip Island, where Captain and Mrs. Denroche reign supreme.

I spoke of Gossip Island as "a haven of rest"—and so it is. It is one of the smallest of the inhabited isles of the Gulf and one of the quaintest. The name is queer to begin with. I'm told it has nothing to do with "gossip" in the ordinary sense of the word. It is a corruption of the name of a former owner—Gossith, or something like that. It is only eighty-three acres in extent, but in that small compass it contains many of the requirements for the ideal holiday. There are a score of little rock-bound bays, and at the head of half a dozen of them, isolated from the others, are summer cottages. There is good bathing in nearly all these bays, and boats are available for fishing or exploring the coastline. Then there is a small hotel on the south-eastern point of the island and two tennis courts. So if you want to be alone with the family for your holiday, where the kids can bathe and amuse themselves with a boat in safety, or if you want tennis and community life at a country hotel—you can have that too. It is really rather a unique place—this Gossip Island.

In the morning we walked all around the "kingdom" by a trail along the rocks, admired the glorious views of the mainland mountains, drank in the beauty and perfume of the woods carpeted with many varieties of wild flowers, and set out later in a launch for Pender Island. The whole Denroche establishment accompanied us—including two small irrepressible sons of the house, who shot scores of gulls with pop-guns and gave me several bad attacks of heart failure when they failed to obey the parental injunction to "Sit still !" It was two o'clock before we reached Port Washington, after a somewhat stormy voyage. There I bade farewell to my kind host and hostess and the small fire-eaters and, shouldering my pack, made my way to Mrs. Logan's at Grosvenor House in search of food.

Pender Island is well supplied with stopping-places of one kind or another, and at Grosvenor House, just near the wharf, I found the first of them. Bill Logan and his wife came here from Penge, near London, eighteen years ago. I smiled when Mrs. Logan told me of their arrival there. They followed some friends—Mr. and Mrs. John McKinnon, who live on James Point across the bay—and one can picture their forlornness when they reached this isolated spot. It was pathetically humorous to hear Mrs. Logan tell of their bewilderment to find no " shops," no "streets," and scarcely any neighbours. They are content enough to-day, however—like so many others who are bewildered at first in a new country.

Someone had told me I must not fail to see Spencer Percival if I visited Pender Island, so I made my way down a precipitous path to the shore, where I found Mr. Percival busily engaged in painting a boat. The tide was rising fast, and he had to complete his job in a limited time, so my call was brief, but it was worth while. Every poultry-man in British Columbia is familiar with his name, for he made a great reputation as a White Wyandotte man and, furthermore, as a fruit-grower on a small scale. Twenty-four years he has been on Pender Island, and his house, surrounded by fruit trees in full blossom, was a sight to gladden wearied eyes. "The finest pears in the world are grown here, sir—without exception"—these were Spencer Percival's last words to me.

There are seventeen miles of good roads on Pender Island, and one of these I now followed across the island to Hope Bay, where is one of the chief settlements. There is the store of the Corbetts, father and son, and it is also a port of call for the island steamers. I was interested in the case of Mr. Corbett senior, as an example of the health-giving qualities of these islands. It appears that when he first came to Pender from Eastern Canada some twenty-five years ago, he was in the worst physical condition; so ill was he that doctors almost despaired of saving his life. To-day, and almost ever since his arrival, he has been active and alert, and there are many useful years yet before him.

Not far away is the farm of another old-timer, whose career is of interest. It is that of Thomas Menzies. I can't be certain of exact dates, but about thirty years ago young Tom Menzies arrived in New Westminster from Eastern Canada. He was broke and needed a job in the worst way. Then he came in touch with the Rev. Ebenezer Robson, a famous old Methodist pioneer of that day. A mission-station was just started on Pender Island, and a man was needed to look after the small bit of a farm there. Tom Menzies was offered the job at a salary of $200 a year, and if he was satisfactory, he was to be given a piece of land as well at the end of his time. In a few months there were doubts as to whether the salary could be paid, and Menzies was given his land there and then. That was the beginning of the fine farm of to-day at Hope Bay, where Tom Menzies has made a name for himself as a breeder of Jersey cattle.

Supper-time found me weary and hungry on the door-step of "Waterlea," a delightful old-world farmhouse where Captain and Mrs. A. E. Craddock make their home. I had covered a good ten miles before I came to this hospitable threshold. It is one of the most lovely spots imaginable. The house is set amid lawns and fruit trees, facing the west. Steamers to and from Victoria and Vancouver pass within a few hundred yards of it. Port Washington is the nearest port of call, two and one-half miles by road. There are tennis courts and a small dancing-room in the grounds, and all round are little rocky bays, one of which provides a fine sandy bathing-beach.

Half a mile away, high up on James Point, is a little cottage standing out from the trees like a look-out station. After supper I made my way up there to call on Mr. and Mrs. John McKinnon, who have made their home here for twenty-three years. In this little home I found once again the answer to the question, "Why do people live on these islands?" for when I put that question to John McKinnon he just said simply, "Well, why not? We are content. We are happy here !" —and really, there seemed no more to be said. What's the use of being facetious in the face of such contentment ! Over the fire-place I noticed a very fine hand-carved mantel and was amazed to learn that this, and the hammered-copper screen beneath it, were the work of Mr. McKinnon, as well as some extremely handsome carved panels elsewhere in the little parlour.

Mr. and Mrs. McKinnon are " Scots frae London toon," but before they took up their abode here, Mr. McKinnon had travelled round the world, and had been far up the mysterious Amazon River. An interesting man, with tales to tell of many lands.

I was stupid enough to ask Mr. McKinnon if he had been able all those years to make a living off his land and with work nearby. "How else would I have lived ?" he replied. "Certainly I have made a living—I have had no other means."

When you ask these islanders how often they go to town, they scratch their heads and try to figure out the last time they saw the "bright lights." Some of them have not been to a city for years; while others occasionally make the journey to Victoria or Vancouver. Victoria, at one time, had most of the business of the Gulf Islands, but more and more they look to Vancouver as their trading centre and chief market.

As you walk along the lanes of Pender Island you constantly hear the clucking of pheasants and often put them up from the side of the road. There are deer, too, in numbers. They tell a story on Pender of a certain Cockney settler who was a faithful church-warden, and who felt that, in view of his regular attendance at church, he should be spared the depredations of deer in his orchard.

"Me—the churchwarden, mind you," he said, "attending church every blooming Sunday, and then to think them blinkin' deer come over and ruin my fruit trees. 'Tain't justice, I says !"

I haven't attempted to tell all about Pender Island—it would require a volume to do that. All I can do is to give an outline of these islands. There are a number of other delightful places to stay at on Pender that I had not time to visit. There is Sunset View House at Hope Bay, and Roesland Farm at Otter Bay, and probably others. All of them have their own individual attractions.

Last , but by no means least, of my calls on Pender Island, I went to see Mr. and Mrs. Washington Grimmer. In Washington Grimmer, hale and hearty on his seventy-sixth birthday on April 26th this year, I met another example of the splendid longevity of the Gulf Islanders. Mr. and Mrs. Grimmer have, I suppose, more or less "retired"—if you can ever use this term in its ordinary sense of a farmer. They live in a pretty bungalow with a little gem of a garden surrounding it looking out over Grimmer's Bay. Within two or three miles of them, on farms which were cleared by the brawn and zeal of the family, live their three sons and two married daughters with their husbands—surely a remarkable record in these days of divided households. The name Grimmer is well known among stockmen all over British Columbia, for the Grimmer Jerseys are famous. The eldest son, an authority on Jersey stock, rejoices in the strange name of Neptune Navy Grimmer— and the reason for this is more astounding than the name itself. He was born in a row-boat in Navy Channel, while his mother was being rowed across to Vancouver Island in expectation of his arrival! The name is appropriate in the circumstances.

Washington Grimmer came to British Columbia forty-seven years ago. He sailed from San Francisco in the first-class section of the ship in which the late Premier, John Oliver, was travelling steerage on his first advent to British Columbia. Also on that ship were Mr. H. J. Cambie, Harry Abbott, Mr. Keefer and other Canadian Pacific Railway surveyors and engineers. But Mr. Grimmer was not then coming from England, his birthplace. He left the Old Country at eighteen months of age for Australia, and lived for many years on Hindmarsh Island in a pioneering community. He has been back to the Old Country of recent years with some members of his family, and he'll tell you that he doesn't regret seventy-five years of pioneering in the least. He's happy and healthy—and what more can one ask of life?

From the busy metropolis of Hope Bay, Pender Island, I took ship—to wit, the S.S. *Otter*, Captain Harris—and crossed, by way of Saturna Island, to Salt Spring Island. Salt Spring Island is a great deal larger than any other island in the group I had been visiting. It contains some 44,000 acres, has been settled in spots for seventy years, boasts 125 miles of good motor roads, has a creamery to which all other islands send their produce, which shipped, in

1926, 130,000 pounds of high-grade butter and, in short, is a highly up-to-date and civilised district. I made the Harbour House at Ganges my headquarters for expeditions to distant parts of this island.

I rolled in here feeling fed up with the rotten weather and generally blue. This hotel is run by a delightful Irish family named Crofton—I say it is run by the whole family, because I could not quite get the hang of them. Mine host was once an efficient member of the battalion with which I left Victoria for the war. He looks about forty, but all my calculations were upset by discovering that the large young man who showed me my room, and whom I judged to be the host's brother, was his son. There were other young men and some charming maidens about, but whether they were the proprietor's aunts and uncles, children or employees, I'm blessed if I know. Anyhow, they made me comfortable, despite my inconvenient arrival in the midst of house-cleaning.

I let the bath overflow and the water ran through the kitchen ceiling apparently—which did not add to my popularity, I fear. No one actually reproved me to my face, but there was an awful racket down below when it happened—much loud shouting and banging on the ceiling—and this I took to be the charming indirect Irish way of asking me to be more careful!

After supper I sallied forth to call on an old acquaintance in the person of W. E. Scott, who is still remembered as a very efficient and popular Deputy Minister of Agriculture of other days. Mr. Scott still farms on a small scale, but long illness has treated him badly in the intervening years. His rock-garden is his pride and was a blaze of beauty.

After sundown I sat on a seat under the trees on the lawn here and swapped reminiscences with my old comrade of the Umpty-Umpth battalion. Ganges lies at the head of a long bay, down the centre of which is a string of tiny narrow islands. At sunset it was a scene of indescribable beauty—quiet and peaceful—and I can well understand why people come here for the summer months from the noisy city. On one of these islands, by the way, is a miniature replica in stone and concrete of a sort of English baronial hall. It stands up proudly on its tiny rocky kingdom, and at the eastern end is a little guard-tower with a slit in it for the archer to shoot arrows through in case the place should be invaded by foes! All very quaint and picturesque and, if I may say so, not altogether out of keeping with some of the unusual people one meets hereabouts.

One of these quaint folk said to me the other day: "You know, my friend, almost everyone on these islands is slightly 'queer' in some direction or other"—and among the "queer" folk he frankly included himself. It all looks so peaceful to the visitor that it is hard to realise that there are bitter feuds between certain factions and families. One whom I met was telling me about one of his neighbours. I asked some innocuous question—"What kind of a man is he?" or something like that. And this was the astonishing reply: "Well, this is the kind of man he is: The more he reads the Bible, the more he drinks, and the more he drinks, the more he beats the kids." I changed the subject for, evidently, I had unwittingly uncovered an old feud.

One morning I left Harbour House early for the north end of the island. I had heard of a darky settlement on Salt Spring, where there are still about fifty people, and I was anxious to visit it. These people, or their forbears, came here as refugees from the South at the time of the Civil War in the 'sixties, and were given land on Salt Spring Island. They live somewhat removed from the white population, and are very little in evidence. At what is known as "The Settlement," about the centre of the island, there is an old cemetery which interested me, for in it were graves, apparently of white men, dating back to 1862 and thereabouts.

I turned north along a side-road, and soon the trail led through thick forest until, as I climbed a hill, I saw below me on the right a farmhouse in a clearing. Outside the back door a comely wench of decidedly dark complexion was singing at her task of washing clothes in a tub.

"Is your father at home?" I called out.

"No," was the decided answer.

"Well, may I come through the gate and take a picture of you?" I asked.

"You'd better not—or I'll call somebody quick," she called back, obviously doubtful of my honesty. So I had to go away without what would have made a very pretty picture.

The road skirted beautiful St. Mary's Lake, one of the nine lakes on the island, said to be full of bass and other fish, and led past much cleared land, where were comfortable farmhouses. About noon I came to Fernwood Farm, where Fred J. James and brothers have their fine seed farm, renting the splendid property from Mr. Charles Lang. Here they grow seeds of every description, from the loveliest flowers to the unlovely onion. The land slopes gently to the east; it has ample water supplies, and with good drainage and long hours of sunshine, the location is said to be ideal for raising seeds. James Brothers have been at this intricate and highly specialised business for ten years or more now, and have built up a fine reputation.

I called on Mr. Lang and his lady, now retired from active work, but keenly interested in all that concerns the welfare and progress of Salt Spring Island. Mr. Lang hails from Cornwall, where he was a contractor in a big way and had other large interests. To him, chiefly, Ganges owes its excellent water supply, brought all the way from Maxwell Lake. Water is not an easy question on most of the islands, but as far as most of Salt Spring is concerned, and particularly Ganges, the problem has been solved by the self-sacrificing investment by Mr. Lang of considerable sums on which he expects but small return for many years.

It was late afternoon when I reached the "estate"—for that is the proper word in this case— of Mr. Henry Bullock, near Ganges. I walked up the drive between high laurel hedges that might have graced an English country-house, and came to the substantial old house. Now I hardly knew what to expect in meeting this famous citizen of Salt Spring, of whom I had heard stories for so many years. Everyone smiles when you mention Mr. Bullock—but it is a kindly affectionate smile.

"Ah, he's a queer one," one man said to me, "but generous and good-hearted—I should say so. Even if he HAS queer notions about some things, this I'll say—no one in need was ever turned away empty-handed from Mr. Bullock. Many a lad has him to thank for kindnesses known only to a few."

And that is a sample of the sort of things they say everywhere about Mr. Bullock. You will note that he is always " Mr." Bullock, for he is regarded with the respect which in rural England is accorded to "The Squire." The story is told of how Mr. Bullock, some years ago, noting the tendency of youths from the Old Country to become slovenly in the matter of clothes, endeavoured to check this tendency by importing a score of top-hats with Eton suits for the smaller lads. To boys who would wear this dignified raiment on Sundays, it is said, the sum of ten or fifteen cents was given. Many in Ganges remember the days when a uniformed page-boy used to run messages to the village from the Bullock residence.

But these stories are told with a kindly smile of days that are gone. Top-hats and Eton suits are not worn by the lads of Salt Spring any more, and I think it would take $100 or more to make them fashionable, even for Sunday wear to-day.

Mr. Bullock has lived on Salt Spring Island for thirty years. His father, a fellow of St. John's College, Oxford, had a college living near Windsor, and perhaps with the beauties of an English country vicarage in mind, Mr. Bullock laid out his grounds at Ganges. At all events, the place reminds one of such a garden—with its tall hedgerows, stately yews and box hedges. In the grounds there is a beautiful lake, of which you can catch a glimpse from the house. Of course, times have changed in thirty years; then, as Mr. Bullock will tell you, you could hire a hard-working Japanese for fifty cents a day—where to-day the wage would be nearly $5—and that makes a difference.

One morning, by the kindness of Mr. Gavin Mouat, one of the pioneer family of that name, whose trading concern has been established on Salt Spring these many years, I was enabled to visit one of the most interesting chicken-farms I have ever seen. This was the farm of Chaplin and Oswald at Vesuvius Bay. It was surprising to learn that from the farm of this man Chaplin—a returned soldier who had never done any chicken-raising before the war—came four out of the twelve exhibition birds which British Columbia sent to the British Empire Exhibition at Wembley.

It is an astonishing place. The partners have had orders from all over the United States and Canada for their eggs and day-old chicks. For day-old chicks they get $30 per hundred, while eggs from their champion Barred Plymouth Rock, known by the unpoetic name of E 10111, have been sold at enormous prices. Five sons of this lady have been sold at $50 each. One of them went to the University of British Columbia; two to California, one to Indiana and one to Syracuse, N.Y. Their shipments of day-old chicks have risen from 500 in 1923 to 7,000 in 1926, and to a probable total of about 14,000 this year—truly an extraordinary record.

I decided to walk from Ganges to Fulford Harbour, where I heard I could get a launch to take me across to Sidney, whence I could go by car to Victoria. It was about an eight-mile hike—not very interesting until I came to the lovely valley which runs through the island from Fulford to Burgoyne Bay. One thing, however, aroused my curiosity on the way, and that was the number of small trucks I met on the road taking loads of new-cut lumber to the assembly wharf at Ganges. I learned that the F. M. Singer Lumber Company has ten small portable mills on Salt Spring, buying timber from settlers, cutting it on the ground and hauling it to the assembly wharf, there to be loaded for Vancouver or elsewhere. Some of the old residents of the place strenuously object to the noise and nuisance of having these trucks rushing all over the place. But as this concern has a monthly pay-roll of $12,500 and cut about 11,000,000 feet of timber last year, it is probable that the settlers find the business a boon.

Near the end of my walk I came to a spot where a rustic bridge crossed a babbling brook. Looking down a grassy bank, where woodland flowers poked their heads up to the sunshine, I saw a miniature spillway and a tiny pond. A few yards farther on, through an ivy-covered gateway, I caught a glimpse of a most lovely garden ablaze with flowers. I heard a voice calling the chickens to supper and so, entering the gate, I met John Carter Mollet, eighty-one years old in March last, and still in love with every flower in his garden.

He took me round the well-kept beds. "You seem to love your garden!" said I. "My garden? It is my life," he said earnestly. " I work from five in the morning till dark, and I am never done with the flowers!" Then, his snow-white hair and beard and his battered hat making him a quaint old figure, he took me to see his water-ram—a simple device by which he controls all the water he needs from his never-dry spring.

I asked John Carter Mollet when and why he came to Canada. He told me he came to Canada from Jersey in 1862. Five years he lived in Ontario, then for a time in the United States, and thirty years ago he settled on Salt Spring.

"But what brought your family out here?" I pursued. And instantly he answered: "Mr. Friend's panorama of Canada. Talk about your 'movies'—why, they are nothing as compared with the vivid panoramas of the old days. Why, I have seen panoramas that have LIVED—like that of Garibaldi's campaigns which I saw seventy years ago. Yes—Mr. Friend's panorama of Ontario and the Maritimes persuaded my father that Canada was the country for him." And this brought to my mind also, amazingly vivid panoramas I had seen as a child in Switzerland and France of the Franco-Prussian War, and I can understand that in the far-off days before "movies," a panorama would have been wonderful immigration propaganda.

We stood and chatted awhile at the gate, and he gave me a buttonhole of pansies. Then he said: "Well, young man, I must go to my chickens. I've been living all alone for fourteen years, you know, and I'm busy. Good-bye—and come and see the old man's garden if you pass this way again."

So I came to my journey's end at Fulford Harbour. I supped in royal style at the "White House" which, despite the name, is a comfortable small hotel in a lovely quiet spot. And late that night I reached Victoria—tired out, minus seven pounds of unnecessary flesh and with mind and body reinvigorated by a delightful stay in these "Summer Isles of Eden."

SIX

The Logging Coast

by Martin Allerdale Grainger

As you walk down Cordova Street in the city of Vancouver you notice a gradual change in the appearance of the shop windows. The shoe stores, drug stores, clothing stores, phonograph stores cease to bother you with their blinding light. You see fewer goods fit for a bank clerk or man in business; you leave "high tone" behind you.

You come to shops that show faller's axes, swamper's axes, single-bitted, double-bitted; screw jacks and pump jacks, wedges, sledge-hammers, and great seven-foot saws with enormous shark teeth, and huge augers for boring boomsticks, looking like properties from a pantomime workshop.

Leckie calls attention to his logging boot, whose bristling spikes are guaranteed to stay in. Clarke exhibits his Wet Proof Peccary Hogskin gloves, that will save your hands when you work with wire ropes. Dungaree trousers are shown to be copper-riveted at the places where a man strains them in working. Then there are oilskins and blankets and rough suits of frieze for winter wear, and woollen mitts.

Outside the shop windows, on the pavement in the street, there is a change in the people too. You see few women. Men look into the windows; men drift up and down the street; men lounge in groups upon the curb. Your eye is struck at once by the unusual proportion of big men in the crowd, men that look powerful even in their town clothes.

Many of these fellows are faultlessly dressed: very new boots, new black clothes of quality, superfine black shirt, black felt hat. A few wear collars.

Others are in rumpled clothes that have been slept in; others, again, in old suits and sweaters; here and there one in dungarees and working boots. You are among loggers.

They are passing time, passing the hours of the days of their trip to town. They chew tobacco, and chew and chew and expectorate, and look across the street and watch any moving thing. At intervals they will exchange remarks impassively; or stand grouped, hands in pockets, two or three men together in gentle, long-drawn-out conversations. They seem to feel the day is passing slowly; they have the air of ocean passengers who watch the lagging clock from meal-time to meal-time with weary effort. For comfort it seems they have divided the long day into reasonable short periods; at the end of each 'tis " time to comeanavadrink." You overhear the invitations as you pass.

Now, as you walk down the street, you see how shops are giving place to saloons and restaurants, and the price of beer decorates each building's front. And you pass the blackboards of employment offices and read chalked thereon:-

"50 axemen wanted at Alberni

5 rigging slingers $4

buckers $31/2, swampers $3."

And you look into the public rooms of hotels that are flush with the street as if they were shop windows; and men sit there watching the passing crowd, chairs tipped back, feet on window-frame, spittoons handy.

You hear a shout or two and noisy laughter, and walk awhile outside the kerb, giving wide berth to a group of men scuffling with one another in alcohol-inspired play. They show activity.

Then your eye catches the name-board of a saloon, and you

remember a paragraph in the morning's paper—

"In a row last night at the Terminus Saloon several men . . ."
and it occurs to you that the chucker-out of a loggers' saloon must
be a man "highly qualified."

* * *

The *Cassiar* sails from the wharf across the railway yard Mon-
days and Thursdays at 8 p.m. It's only a short step from the Gold
House and the Terminus and the other hotels, and a big bunch of
the boys generally comes down to see the boat off.

You attend a sort of social function. You make a pleasing break
in the monotony of drifting up the street to the Terminus and down
the street to the Eureka, and having a drink with the crowd in the
Columbia bar, and standing drinks to the girls at number so-and-so
Dupont Street, the monotony that makes up your holiday in Vancouver. Besides, if you are a *woodsman* you will see fellow aristo-
crats who are going north to jobs: you maintain your elaborate
knowledge of what is going on in the woods and where every one
is; and, further, you know that in many a hotel and logging-camp
up the coast new arrivals from town will shortly be mentioning,
casual-like: "Jimmy Jones was down to the wharf night before last.
Been blowing-her-in in great shape has Jimmy, round them saloons.
Guess he'll be broke and hunting a job in about another week, the
pace he's goin' now."

You have informed the *Morning Post!*

If logging is but the chief among your twenty trades and profes-
sions— you are just the ordinary western *logger* —still the north-
going *Cassiar* has great interest for you. Even your friend Tennes-
see, who would hesitate whether to say telegraph operator or car-
penter if you asked him his business suddenly—even he may want
to keep watch over the way things are going in the logging world.

So you all hang around on the wharf and see who goes on
board, and where they're going to, and what wages they hired on
at. And perhaps you'll help a perfect stranger to get himself and
two bottles of whisky (by way of baggage) up the gang-plank; and
help throw Mike McCurdy into the cargo-room, and his blankets
after him.

Then the *Cassiar* pulls out amid cheers and shouted messages,
and you return up town to make a round of the bars, and you laugh

once in a while to find some paralysed passenger whom friends had forgotten to put aboard. . . . And so to bed.

* * *

The first thing a fellow needs when he hits Vancouver is a clean-up: hair cut, shave, and perhaps a bath. Then he'll want a new hat for sure. The suit of town clothes that, stuffed into the bottom of a canvas bag, has travelled around with him for weeks or months—sometimes wetted in rowboats, sometimes crumpled into a seat or pillow—the suit may be too shabby. So a fellow will feel the wad of bills in his pocket and decide whether it's worth getting a new suit or not.

The next thing is to fix on a stopping-place. Some men take a fifty-cent room in a rooming house and feed in the restaurants. The great objection to that is the uncertainty of getting home at night. In boom times I have known men of a romantic disposition who took lodgings in those houses where champagne is kept on the premises and where there is a certain society. But that means frenzied finance, and this time you and I are not going to play the fool and blow in our little stake same as we did last visit to Vancouver.

So a fellow can't do better than go to a good, respectable hotel where he knows the proprietor and the bar-tenders, and where there are some decent men stopping. Then he knows he will be looked after when he is drunk; and getting drunk, he will not be distressed by spasms of anxiety lest some one should go through his pockets and leave him broke. There are some shady characters in a town like Vancouver, and persons of the under-world.

Of course, the first two days in town a man will get good-and-drunk. That is all right, as any doctor will tell you; that is good for a fellow after hard days and weeks of work in the woods.

But you and I are no drinking men, and we stop there and sober up. We sit round the stove in the hotel and read the newspapers, and discuss Roosevelt, and the Trusts, and Socialism, and Japanese immigration; and we tell yarns and talk logs. We sit at the window and watch the street. The hotel bar is in the next room, and we rise once in a while and take a party in to "haveadrink." The bar-tender is a good fellow, one of the boys: he puts up the drinks himself, and we feel the hospitality of it. We make a genial group. Conversation will be about loggers and logs, of course, but in light anecdotal vein, with loud bursts of laughter.

Now one or two of the friends you meet are on the bust; ceaselessly setting-up the drinks, insisting that everybody drink with them. I am not "drinking" myself: I take a cigar and fade away. But you stay; politeness and good fellowship demand that you should join each wave that goes up to the bar, and when good men are spending money you would be mean not to spend yours too. . . .

Pretty soon you feel the sweet reasonableness of it all. A hardworking man should indemnify himself for past hardships. He owes it to himself to have a hobby of some kind. You indulge a hobby for whisky.

About this time it is as well to hand over your roll of bills to Jimmy Ross, the proprietor. Then you don't have to bother with money any more: you just wave your hand each time to the bartender. He will keep track of what you spend. . . .

Now you are fairly on the bust: friends all round you, good boys all. Some are hard up, and you tell Jimmy to give them five or ten dollars; and, "Gimme ten or twenty," you'll say, " I want to take a look round the saloons"—which you do with a retinue.

The great point now is never to let yourself get sober. You'll feel awful sick if you do. By keeping good-and-drunk you keep joyous. "Look bad but feel good" is sound sentiment. Even suppose you were so drunk last night that Bob Doherty knocked the stuffing out of you in the Eureka bar, and you have a rankling feeling that your reputation as a fighting man has suffered somewhat —still, never mind, line up, boys; whisky for mine: let her whoop, and to hell with care! Yah-hurrup and smash the glass!!

If you are " acquainted" with Jimmy Ross—that is to say, if you have blown in one or two cheques before at his place, and if he knows you as a competent woodsman—Jimmy will just reach down in his pocket and lend you fives and tens after your own money is all gone. In this way you can keep on the bust a little longer, and ease off gradually—keeping pace with Jimmy's growing disinclination to lend. But sooner or later you've got to face the fact that the time has come to hunt another job.

There will be some boss loggers in town; you may have been drinking with them. Some of them perhaps will be sobering up and beginning to remember the business that brought them to Vancouver, and to think of their neglected camps up-coast.

Boss loggers generally want men; here are chances for you. Again, Jimmy Ross may be acting as a sort of agent for some of the northern logging-camps: if you're any good Jimmy may send you up to a camp. Employment offices, of course, are below contempt—they are for men strange to the country, incompetents, labourers, farm hands, and the like.

You make inquiries round the saloons. In the Eureka some one introduces you to Wallace Campbell. He wants a riggin' slinger: you are a riggin' slinger. Wallace eyes the bleary wreck you look. Long practice tells him what sort of a man you probably are when you're in health. He stands the drinks, hires you at four and a half, and that night you find yourself, singing drunk, in the *Cassiar's* saloon—on your way north to work.

* * *

I was not singing drunk myself, nor was I on my way to securely promised work, as I stood upon the deck of the steamer *Cassiar* one evening and watched the lights of Vancouver disappear. In fact, I was depressingly sober, as it is my habit to be; and I began to think with some anxiety of my immediate affairs and to make a series of hurried calculations.

My steamer fare had cost five dollars and a half. But there was a pound of cheese and two packets of grape-nuts in my bag, and so I knew I could avoid the fifty-cent meals aboard the boat. Thus Friday night would see me landed at Hanson Island Hotel with sixteen dollars and a half in pocket.

Now on what system did they run that hotel? What would they charge? Meals would be fifty cents; that I knew. But would they throw in sleeping accommodation—bed or floor—free gratis as at Port Browning? If so, I could allow myself to eat two meals a day, and so last out for eleven days, and still have five and a half dollars for the return trip to Vancouver should that be necessary.

"Why all these considerations?" you will ask. "Why think of the return journey?"

Well, you see, my prospects were uncertain. Two months had gone since Carter had asked me to work for him. Carter might have changed his mind. Carter might be ill. Carter might have decided to shut down camp this winter. And so at Hanson Island I might find myself among strangers, with no one to give me work. Indeed, all sorts of unpleasant things might happen. I had left my last job and been laid up for several weeks on account of a damaged foot; and the foot was still troublesome. And so I could not venture to undertake any work that should require real activity. There were thus few jobs possible for me in that logging country.

Then, again, suppose Carter's steamboat should not come down from the camp to Hanson Island for one week, two weeks, three weeks. I couldn't sit on the hotel veranda for three solid weeks. Besides, I would not have the money to do it. And I felt I would be too shy to explain the situation to the hotel proprietor. It was not as if I had the certainty of work when Carter's steamer should arrive. Had I that, it would be easy to tell the hotel man to charge up my expenses to my boss. But as an utter stranger, with no certain job in view, how could I ask for credit? Jawbone is the western word for credit. I lack the art of using mine persuasively.

So it looked much as if I should have to turn tail and leave the logging country unless Carter or his boat should turn up at Hanson Island within ten days, or unless, of course, I could strike another job that would suit a man with a damaged foot. After all, Hanson Island might be in some ways an eligible centre for business purposes. . . . So I meditated; and then fell into conversation with an old fellow who, like me, preferred the open deck to the noise and stuffiness of the crowded saloon. We listened to the slap of the ripples against the steamer's bow as she thumped her way up the Gulf, and we looked into the darkness. The old fellow told me a great yarn of the early days on San Juan Island; and of how the shooting of Fluit's pigs by Cutler nearly led to war between British Columbia and the State of Washington somewhere in the 'sixties or early 'seventies; and of how, when garrisons were placed by either party on the island, he and his brother had found an opening for an ingenious system of smuggling and had made money.

The wind began to feel cold and we went inside the saloon. The boat was really very quiet now. In the smoking-room there sat a coterie engaged at whisky, but at the stern their bursts of laughter and loud talk were made remote by the steady throbbing from the engine-room and by the snores of sleeping men. There was no temptation to waste money on a berth, for all the little cabins were taken and several men were sleeping on the passage floors. By good luck I found a bench unoccupied, and lying down, drew some oil-skins over me and set myself to sleep. Some time in the night I remember a gentleman lifting off my covering and looking at my face. He was speechlessly drunk, I think, and he patted my head. I think I fell asleep while he was doing it. . . . Next morning I awoke to eat my cheese and grape-nuts and to look upon a glorious dawn. The sea, in the narrow channels that we threaded, was glassy calm; except where our churning wake lay white behind us, and where the steamer's bows sent a small swell to swash against the near-by rocks. There is deep water close to shore almost everywhere along the coast.

If you take a large scale map of British Columbia you will notice how the three-hundred-mile stretch of Vancouver Island, like a great breakwater, shuts off from the ocean a fine strip of sea, and how that sea is all littered with islands. You will see the outline of the mainland coast, from Vancouver north, a jagged outline all dented with inlets and sounds and arms—fiords they call them elsewhere. Try to realise that the shores of these fiords are mostly mountain slopes, that slopes and narrow valleys and hilly islands—all the land everywhere—are covered with big forest to the very edge of tide-water, and you will have some idea of the scenery I looked upon that morning from the after-deck of the *Cassiar*.

There was green forest—and it looked like a moss upon the higher slopes; and the bristling dead poles of burnt forest showing against the bare mottled rock: standing timber, fallen timber, floating logs and tree tops; and drift logs piled white upon the beach. There were long stretches of coast along which, every few yards, little lanes seemed to have been cut in the water-side forest. And now we were well into the northern logging country; for these little lanes marked the work of hand-loggers, and were the paths down which big logs had crashed their way into the sea.

I let the scenery be and wandered round the ship, watching, under cover of a bored demeanour, my fellow passengers. All of us had become quiet and respectable. The bar-room did no business. Some men slept on benches, slept solid; sleeping off the after-effects of Vancouver and "life." Most of us mooned about the deck, in silence; or listened, in groups, to the conversation of those who spoke.

Some of us were obviously not loggers. One man, I think, was a lawyer going up to a camp on some business. There were one or two timber buyers—one I recognised as a man who acts as an agent for a Lumber Company on Broughton Island.

Last summer the timber speculators and pulp-concession men persuaded the authorities to send a police launch cruising round the islands and inlets of the coast: the story was that the hand-loggers were getting logs from timber lands that had been staked—that is to say, that had become private property. The police on the launch collared a number of men and took them down for trial to Vancouver on the charge of stealing. Some of these men were now on board, returning north on bail. One man told us that day how he had been at work with his mate sawing a tree when the policeman came and demanded his licence; and how the policeman wouldn't let him go to his cabin (a few miles away) to fetch it, but had dragged him off then and there. The man talked of suing for damages. There was a boss logger on board who had been obliged to stop work by the police—they said he had been taking logs from a pulp-concession. The quaint thing about this is that a pulp-concession is only granted on lands where there is no timber fit for logging purposes. Some one, one supposes, has had to swear that these lands can yield no logs—and then, a year or so after, hand-loggers are prosecuted for stealing the logs whose existence has been denied!

I know nothing of the other side of the case; but on board that morning men talked freely of "graft" and "political pull." It was held to be shameful that great tracts of country should be closed against the *bona fide* logger and lie idle for the future profit of speculators.

Every now and again we would see the distant roof of a logging-camp shining yellow through the trees, and hear the whistle of a donkey-engine from where white puffs of steam would show against the forest green. Then the *Cassiar* would toot and slow down, and the camp rowboat would put out to intercept us. A whole fleet of hand-loggers' boats would come out too, and tie up to the steamer's side for a few hurried minutes while meat and supplies and mail were being thrown into them. We passengers would all lean over the deck-rail above and laugh at little breakages that would occur to freight, and recognise acquaintances in the boats alongside and shout the latest news from Vancouver to them.

Down on the *Cassiar's* lower deck were rows and rows of huge quarters of beef for the camps, and piles of heavy boom chains and coils of wire cable and groceries galore, in boxes and in sacks. There were new rowboats fresh from the builders in Vancouver, and old rowboats belonging to passengers who were going timber-cruising farther north. The lower deck, in fact, was just a cargo-room, with a space partitioned off to hold the liquor and the bar-tender. Aft of the cargo-room were the oily-smelling engines, and the little rooms where China-men and Japanese cooked and washed dishes and peeled potatoes. There too was the skookum box—that is, the *strong room* or lock-up. To it the first mate of the *Cassiar* is wont to shoot too noisy drunks, pushing them before him, at arm's length, with that fine collar-and-trouserseat grip of his that is so much admired.

Just beyond Church House we lay at anchor for an hour or two, waiting for slack water in the Euclataws. The northern and the southern tides meet here, and in the narrow channel whirlpools form. There's something in the sinister, all-powerful thrust and sweep of such water that puts the fear of God into a man in a rowboat—if he is a little bit late for slack water. But of course the *Cassiar* doesn't mind going through, as long as the tide hasn't turned very long.

The White Frenchman came out in his boat for supplies. In the last month, I notice, he has collected quite a few logs—all lonely himself in that dismal place. For his shack is on the mountain slope just below the rapids: the situation chosen for beach-combing purposes. When a tug towing a raft gets into trouble at the Euclataws and loses logs Auguste is sure to pick up some.

Perhaps it was the monotony of the cheese and grapenuts (eaten within smell of tempting odours from the dining-saloon) that made the day seem dull to me; perhaps it was the vague gnawing unhappiness that a nervous person always feels when facing the uncertainty of getting work; or perhaps it was the poorness of my luck in attempting acquaintance with other men on board. I cut a feeble figure in such casual talk; the men I spoke to seemed to be duller still.

The westerner—especially the American westerner—has usually a composed and competent air. It is surprising sometimes when you have nerved yourself (after some shyness) to commence a conversation with a grim-looking stranger, to find that he is really feeling rather lonely and "out of it" in strange surroundings. There is so often a wonderful contrast between the ease of the man's appearance and the uneasiness that shows in his talk. . . .

I noticed that I broke the ice with about ten men on board, but not a soul took the first step and addressed me. And yet some of the men I tackled proved to be desperately anxious to talk once they had been spoken to. One reason I imagined was that the great demand for men had brought an unusual number of strangers about. Another reason was that one's "twang" and "broadness of speech" and queer way of expressing oneself—the result of an education in England—made one strange and difficult for them to size up.

At eleven o'clock, in the pitch darkness of that Friday night, the *Cassiar* drew near to Hanson Island and made the hilly shores of the narrow channel re-echo with her siren. We passed a dark headland and saw the lights of the hotel.

Several lanterns were flickering about along the beach, and we could judge that men were launching rowboats and hurrying to meet us at the raft. For at Hanson Island there is no wharf. A large raft anchored in the sea serves for the landing-stage; a shed built thereon serves as warehouse for the freight.

The *Cassiar's* searchlight glared upon the raft where men stood waiting to catch the mooring ropes. The steamer edged her way gingerly alongside and was made fast; the doors of the cargo-room were opened, freight was poured out upon the raft, hurriedly; and we passengers let ourselves down upon the boxes and bales that lay piled in rank confusion. All was black shadow, and dim forms and feeble lantern gleams.

I was surprised, for a moment, to find that a man had seized my blanket roll and pitched it into the far darkness; but then I found a boat was waiting there. Some one flashed a lantern; I jumped into the boat. I saw a solemn, fat old Dutchman tumble in behind me; other men came pushing in. Soon in that boat we were a solid mass of men and bundles. Then we began to move, and I heard a weak, drunken voice appealing for more room to work his oars. Heavens! I recognised those wheedling tones at once. The oarsman was my old acquaintance Jim; Jim the "engineer"; Jim, ex-coal-trimmer from the White Star Line.

My old acquaintance Jim was dreadful drunk, but not too drunk to know his duty. He held to a design to row the boat ashore, aiming for where the hotel lights shone bright above the beach. We moved through utter darkness, Jim's oars waggling feebly in the water.

Then we went bump and bump again, and reaching out our hands, we felt a floating log that barred our path. We seemed to get entangled with logs; logs everywhere. Jim, with sudden fury, tried to row over them. Then he gave up the attempt and told us to walk ashore upon the logs. But a tearful-drunk old voice wailed against the idea in foreign-sounding cockney accents, and other voices made an angry chorus, saying that their boots were not spiked and that they would walk no slippery logs in darkness, and they swore. So the engineer became absorbed again in trying to row over logs, bump, bump, bump . . . until he felt it futile and reached the querulous verge of tears. . . . I jumped, thigh-deep, into the water then and took my stuff ashore, leaving the fools in drunken argument.

I opened the front door of the hotel and walked, half blinded by the dazzle of acetylene, into the public room. Noise was my first impression—noise of shuffling feet, stamp of dancing men, loud talk and shouted cuss-words. Then I saw that the room was crowded.

A red-hot stove stood in one corner, and round it men sat in chairs or stood warming themselves or drying their wet clothes. A card game was going on at a small table, and men stood around, three deep, to watch the play. Large sums were in the pool. There was an incessant coming and going of men between the bar-room and the public room, and men loafed about the rooms and passages and talked, or argued, or scuffled playfully. Some danced to the tunes of a fiddle played by an old man who swayed with shut eyes, rapt in his discordant scraping.

In fact, the hotel was doing good business that night. The whirlpool, as a temperance tract might say, was a-booming and a-boiling, sucking down men's wages and perhaps their health; the boys were "on the tear", and the hotel resounded with their revelry. Those who had fallen lay splayed out upon the floor in drunken sleep; those who were sick lay outside in the night. The scene reminded me a little of boating suppers and undergraduates; but the action, of course, was much more vigorous, as befitted grown-up men.

Now I had no idea of the arrangements usual in such places, in a loggers' hotel, and there was no one around to tell me. I quailed before the publicity of confronting the majestic bar-tender at his bar, and drawing the attention of a roomful to my ignorance.

I felt conspicuous, for by some accident I still wore a dirty collar. Men eyed me askance . . . and it was some time before I took my courage in both hands and walked nervously into the kitchen. I asked timidly for a bed (a more tactful word I thought than *room*), and a bar-tender off duty took me up to the second storey—a great loft of a place under the sloping roof—and told me to hunt among the beds until I found what I wanted. "The beds up here are good and clean," he said, with friendly assurance (no lice, he meant). That was all I wanted to know. I realised the situation at once, found a fine clean space of floor beneath an open window, spread my blankets, and turned in.

Gentlemen were breathing stertorously from adjacent beds... and the roar from beneath, and scraping of chairs and shuffling, and the busy hum from the bar, were as the noise of the sea—lulling me to sleep.

SEVEN

Sailing with Vancouver

by William W. Woollen

Burke Channel, as now known, is a long inlet on the east side of Fitzhugh Sound, three miles northward of Namu Harbor. It leads to Bella Coola anchorage, at the head of North Bentinck Arm, a distance of fifty-five miles in a general northeasterly direction, from its junction with Fitzhugh Sound. It lies between high, precipitous rocky mountains, the sides of which are covered with stunted pine trees, and mostly snowcapped, becoming more lofty as the head of the inlet is approached. This channel and arm, though not surveyed in detail, have been frequently traversed both by day and night. I voyaged through them July 13, 1918.

North Bentinck Arm is eight miles long, and just within the entrance, on the north shore, is a small bay affording anchorage for small craft. The head terminates in a sand and mud flat, fronting low swampy ground, covered with grass, which is submerged at high water. Here the inlet is one and three-tenths miles wide. Bella Kula, formerly known as Bella Coola, at the head of North Bentinck Arm, affords an indifferent anchorage close to the sand flat at the mouth of the Bella Kula River, off the wharf on the south side. Small vessels may find shelter, during summer, on the north shore in the cove northward of Custom House Point. Bella Kula River is a stream of considerable size and velocity, the deposit from which has formed a steep bank at the head of the inlet. The water is quite fresh alongside, and if pumped in at low water is fit for drinking. There is a Norwegian settlement on the southern shore of the bay. A long narrow wharf with a depth of sixteen feet or more at its outer end, with several buildings on it, extends from the shore near the settlement. A government wharf is situated on the north side of the entrance to the river. This is the anchorage reached by Mackenzie in 1793. The rock upon which he made the inscription, noting his arrival at this point, has been defaced, the inscription having been obliterated by time. In its place has been cut into the face of the rock the following inscription: "See Appleford 10, Imperial Block, Interior, Vancouver and S." I was told that the man who defaced this historical rock was a real estate agent, who lived at Victoria and operated in that city and Vancouver.

On May 30, Vancouver set out in the yawl, accompanied by Lieutenant Swaine in the cutter, to examine the main arm of Burke Channel. They had not gone far until they landed on some rocks near the western shore, where they were visited by a few of the natives, who appeared to be of a different race from those they had seen to the southward and used a different language to that spoken by the inhabitants of Nootka. Their stature was much more robust than that of the Indians further south. The prominence of their countenances and the regularity of their features resembled those of the northern Europeans; their faces were generally broad, with high cheek bones. Had it not been for the filth, oil, and paint with which from their earliest infancy they had been besmeared from head to foot, there was reason to believe that their color would have differed but little from that of laboring Europeans who were constantly exposed to the alterations of the weather.

On his way back to the ships Vancouver explored Dean Channel. I voyaged through this channel on July 14, 1918. On our way through it, we passed logging camps operated by the Ocean Falls Pulp and Paper Company. The surroundings were impressive; the mountains resembled stone walls covered with ivy. The grotesque marking of the snow on the mountain sides looked like hieroglyphics. At Kinsquit, the place to which Mackenzie came from Bella Coola, are located two canneries and an Indian settlement. Here also is the mouth of Dean River, from the mouth of which is seen on the eastern side a sand bank. Two miles above here the inlet is contracted to about one mile in width by two spits. The bay at the head of the inlet is circular in form. When I was there a railroad, extending into it, had been constructed into the forest. I was informed that logging camp No. 17, which had just been organized, consisted of one hundred and seventy-five men, engaged in logging for the Ocean Falls Pulp and Paper Company. When it is remembered that there were about twenty such camps thus engaged, one gets an idea of the fearful destruction of timber which is now taking place along the various inlets in this section of the country.

To one arm of Dean Channel, Vancouver gave the name of Cascade Channel. It is now known as Cascade Inlet. The width of this channel did not anywhere exceed three-quarters of a mile; its shores were bounded by precipices much more perpendicular than any they had yet seen during this excursion; and from the summits of the mountains that overlooked it, particularly on its northeastern shore, there fell several large cascades. These were exceedingly grand, and much the largest and most tremendous of any the explorers had ever beheld. The impetuosity with which the waters descended produced a strong current of air that reached nearly to the opposite side of the channel, though it was perfectly calm in every other direction.

Near the south point of Cascade Channel they met friendly Indians, who invited them to visit their habitations, and the invitation was accepted. They found the village to consist of seven houses situated in a small rocky cove close round the point. On approaching the dwellings the Indians desired that they would not land there, but on the opposite side of the cove. This Vancouver's party did and by so doing secured their confidence. They were visited by about forty of the male inhabitants, but the women and children remained in their houses. The construction of these were very curious. The back parts of them appeared to be supported by the projection of a very high, and nearly perpendicular rocky cliff and the front and sides by slender poles, about sixteen or eighteen feet high. Vancouver desired to become better acquainted with these curious mansions, but the repugnance shown by their owners to his entering them, induced him not to make the attempt lest it might give them serious offense and disturb the harmony that existed. Not one of them had a weapon of any kind, and they all conducted themselves in the most civil and orderly manner.

In Hakai Passage the explorers passed close to a rock on which another native village was situated. The rock appeared to be about half a mile in circuit and was entirely occupied by the habitations of the natives. These appeared to be well constructed; the boards forming the sides of the houses were well fitted, and the roofs rose from each side with sufficient inclination to throw off the rain. The gable ends were decorated with curious paintings, and near one or two of the most conspicuous mansions were carved figures in large logs of timber (evidently totems) representing a gigantic human form, with strange and uncommonly distorted features. The Indians made objections to Vancouver and his party landing. Their number amounted at least to three hundred. After being gratified with some presents, they returned to their rock, and the party continued their route homeward.

About noon of June 8, in a bay opposite an opening on the western shore that had the appearance of communicating with the ocean, the explorers fell in with about forty native men, women, and children. The natives received them with caution and desired that they land at a rock a little distant from their party. On complying, they were visited by most of the women and boys, who, after receiving some presents, gave them to understand that the women would have no objection to their company, but Vancouver declined their solicitations. The whole of this party were employed in gathering cockles and in preparing a sort of paste from the inner bark of a particular kind of pine tree, intended as a substitute for bread. This they washed in sea water, beat it very hard on the rocks, and then made it up into balls. It had a sweetish taste, was very tender, and by them seemed to be considered good food. About ten o'clock at night, the explorers arrived on ship board and found all well. During Vancouver's absence some excellent spruce beer had been brewed from the trees found in that locality, and a sufficient supply of fish for the use of all for every day had been procured.

* * *

On McLoughlin Bay on the west side of Lama Passage is the site of an old Hudson's Bay trading post. The Bella Bella Indians migrated here from Bella Bella Islands in 1868. This village is called New Bella Bella, in contra-distinction of the former home of these Indians. Captain Nord of the steamship *Jefferson* in a letter to me says: "I understand the reason for moving the town from the old town site was due to the fact that the Hudson's Bay Company had established a store at old Bella Bella and the Indians considered the prices charged by the Company for supplies to be exorbitant and the natives moved to the westward and there established a new town." In a letter from Captain L. F. Lock of the steamship *Princess Alice*, he says: "I am well acquainted with the fact that at one time they were located at McLoughlin Bay, just outside of the Reserve. One John Clayton opened a store at that place, bought all the townsite from the government, and tried to compel the Indians to pay rent or buy the lots they were living on. This they would not do, so they left the old town and moved about three miles further away and on the Reservation, where they still remain."

The Bella Bellas in their new home, through the efforts of the missionaries, have become an orderly, industrious, thrifty, self-supporting, and christianized People. Near their town along the shore is their graveyard with wooden tombs, painted with totemic designs, and flags and streamers flying from tall poles. Across Lama Passage from Bella Bella on the continent is an old Indian burial place, a wild and romantic spot, close on the edge of the water. Great boulders of fantastic shapes stand all about, draped with loose thick moss so highly colored and mixed with various tints of green as to challenge an artist's cunning to produce their harmonious combination. The trees are tall and sombre and stand as nature planted them where others of their kind have stood and fallen and decayed in the ages gone before.

During June 10-17, a boat party under Mr. Johnstone explored Portlock Channel. They saw a number of natives but found all of them friendly. One morning, they stopped in a small cove for breakfast. Finding some mussels, some of the men roasted and ate a number, as had been a usual practice when any of these bivalves were discovered. Soon after they quitted the cove, several of the men who had eaten the mussels were seized with a numbness about their faces and extremities; their whole bodies were shortly affected in the same manner, attended with sickness and giddiness. Mr. Barrie, who commanded one of the boats, had, when in England, experienced a similar disaster from the same cause and was himself indisposed on the present occasion. Recollecting that he had received great relief by violent perspiration, he took an oar and earnestly advised those who were unwell, viz, John Carter, John McAlpin, and John Thomas, to use their utmost exertion in order to throw themselves into a profuse perspiration; this Mr. Barrie affected in himself and found considerable relief, but when the party landed for dinner, and their exertions at the oars ceased, the three seamen were obliged to be carried on shore. Mr. Johnstone ordered warm water to be immediately gotten ready in the hope that by copiously drinking the same, the offending matter might be removed. Carter, however, was unable to swallow the water and he expired about a half an hour after he was landed. His death was so tranquil that it was no doubt that it was occasioned by a poison contained in the mussels he had eaten. When he was first taken ill, his pulse was regular but it gradually grew fainter and weaker until he expired, when his lips turned black, and his hands, face, and neck were much swollen. Such was the foolish obstinacy of the others who were affected, that it was not until this poor unfortunate fellow resigned his life, that they could be prevailed upon to drink the hot water; his fate, however, induced them to follow the advice of their officer, and the desired effect being produced they all obtained relief. This very unexpected and unfortunate circumstance detained the boats about three hours; when, having taken the corpse on board and refreshed the three sick men with some warm tea and having covered them up warm in the boat, they continued their route down Sheep Passage, the southwest channel, until they stopped in a bay for the night, where they buried the dead body. To this Vancouver gave the name of Carter's Bay, after the unfortunate fellow. To distinguish the fatal spot where the mussels were eaten he called the place Poison Cove and the branch leading to it Mussel Channel.

* * *

From the north end of Douglas Channel the inlet continues in a northerly direction for a further distance of about seventeen miles and is terminated by a border of low land with a shallow flat extending from side to side, through which a stream discharges at the northeastern corner, navigable only for canoes. This head of the inlet is known as the Kitimat Arm. Its termination differs in some respects from many of the others; its shores are not very abrupt but are bounded on each side by a range of lofty mountains, which, however, are not, as is generally the case, connected at the head of the arm but continue apparently in a direction parallel to each other. The valley between them, which is three or four miles wide, is covered with trees, mostly of the pine variety. An Indian village of the Kitimat tribe is situated near the head of this arm on the eastern shore, with a mission, town hall, and store.

On July 2, the ships quitted their anchorage on Klekane Inlet and proceeded to a new one, while boat parties were again sent out to explore. A party under Mr. Whidbey surveyed Douglas Channel, passed through Grenville Channel, and visited many other places, including Chatham Sound and Pitt's Archipelago.

I have voyaged through Grenville Channel ten times. It was so named by Vancouver after the Right Honorable Lord Grenville. It is forty-five miles long and is the channel which steam vessels take when proceeding by inshore passage to Chatham Sound, Prince Rupert Harbor, and other northwestern points. Ogden Channel, from the sea, joins it abreast of Gibson Island in the northern entrance. Its entrance eastward of Farrant Island is from eight to ten cables wide, which is gradually reduced to about three cables as Lowe Inlet is approached some twelve miles up, from whence it continues about that width until northward of Point Evening, Klewnuggit Inlet. Above this point Grenville Channel gradually widens and is about two miles wide abreast of Point Calvert, on the west side of the northern entrance. The depths of most parts of it are about fifty fathoms. The land on both sides of the channel is high, reaching an elevation of three thousand five hundred feet on the northeast, and from one thousand to two thousand feet on the southwestern shore, and for the most part is densely wooded with pine and cedar trees. The mountains rise almost perpendicularly from the water, and cause the southern portion of the narrow channel to appear even more narrow than it is. This "deep, glass-floored, echoing green lane" is perhaps the most magnificent waterway on the Inside Passage. Here the eye and ear are greeted with steep forest-clad mountain ranges hardly a quarter of a mile apart, snow-clad crags, the tracks of snow and rock slides, hanging valleys, and noisy waterfalls, sometimes dancing down from the highest peaks in one uninterrupted leap. Its waters are clear, washed green, in which are reflected the wonderful scenery of its shores.

Whidbey's party surveyed the waters in the neighborhood of Raspberry Islands, and from the rapidity and regularity of the tide began to suspect the inlet "to be a river." But they did not investigate further and failed to discover that they were in the estuary of the Skeena River, the largest stream on the coast of British Columbia north of the Fraser.

The name Skeena is taken from "*Skee,* terror, calamity, trouble; and *Kena,* a stream.*" It is said the name was given to it because of its poisonous shell fish, which killed many canoe loads of the first people who came around from the Nass River and entered it. It is navigable by small steamers for sixty miles above its mouth and for two hundred miles by canoes. It is the greatest salmon stream on the northwest coast. The word "Tsimpsean" means "in the Skeena," by which is meant to express: "The people living on or along the banks of the Skeena River," and this correctly records a historical fact, for the Tsimpsean tribes, many generations ago, lived at different points along the banks of the Skeena River. The name of each tribe gives those acquainted with the topography of the country, and the language, the exact original location of all the tribes.

In July, the Tsimpseans return from the Nass River to their old fishing villages on the Skeena River, where for centuries their ancestors have exercised the privilege of catching the red salmon as it is wriggling its way up to its breeding ground to deposit its spawn. Here, in a few weeks, not only all necessary fish for immediate use, but a full supply for the remainder of the year, as well as for trading purposes, is secured; the whole family turns its attention towards picking and drying the wild berries growing in abundance along the banks of the river, as well as to the curing of the salmon caught by smoking and drying it for use. There is perhaps, the most remarkable display of totem poles along this river to be found on the northwest coast. The empire of the Kwakutle Indian ceases at the mouth of the Skeena River, and the Tsimpsean, the greatest of the coast tribes, occupy the coast to the Alaska line. These Indians have always held a monopoly of the inland land, maintained a trail with the interior, and kept the Tinnehs in admirable subjection. A few of these mountaineers are occasionally seen on the river. This explains why Fort Stager and Hazelton continued so long to be mentioned as stockaded posts by the Hudson's Bay Company. Surrounding the mouth of the Skeena River are canneries at Port Essington, Claxton, Cascade, Aberdeen, Inverness, Standard, and Mumford Landing, the work at and for which is performed by Indians, Chinese, Japanese, Greeks, and Scandinavians. One of the most beautiful sights that I have seen was that of hundreds of these fishermen casting nets in these waters.

The town of Port Essington lies on the south shore of Skeena River about thirteen miles from its mouth and six miles from De Horsey Island. The village is situated on the west side of Point Village, forming the angle between the Skeena and Estall rivers. There are two wharves, a post office, and two churches here. This is an important distributing station for the British Columbia hinterland, and it is a center of fishing and tanning industries. It is distant from Hazelton, the head of Skeena River navigation, one hundred and forty-five miles. Balmoral settlement lies on the east side of the mouth of Estall River. Steam vessels call regularly at the large cannery at Balmoral. Raspberry Islands lie off the east point of Estall River, northwest of Balmoral; they consist of two wooded islets joined together at low water. At two miles above Raspberry Islands, on the southern shore, is a hot spring; the inhabitants use it for rheumatic affections. Potatoes are plentiful; also berries, which are dried by the Indians for winter food.

On July 4, the ships left their anchorage and proceeded to a new rendezvous in an inlet on the east side of the Isle de Gil. Here they remained a few days and, on the 9th, moved to a place called Fisherman's Cove on the coast of the same island. Here the crews feasted on fish taken with the seine and on berries picked on the shore. Here also they were visited by three canoes of natives, who seemed to Vancouver to differ somewhat in appearance from the Indians thus far seen.

On July 14, the ships quitted Fisherman's Cove and in the evening passed through Otter Channel, the northern entrance into Nepean Sound, when the wind, which blew in very light air, being favorable, their course was directed slowly up the Canal del Principe.

A Great River North: II

Pledged to Neptune

by Kathrene Pinkerton

There's a great advantage in starting a new experience at scratch. Then one has no set conditions by which to measure. So I looked with awed wonder at the compactness and versatility of the *Yakima's* arrangements. The small cabin was transformed into a dining room by merely letting down a hinged table from a bulkhead, and converted into sleeping quarters at night by lifting up the backs of the transom berths. Lockers held the bedding, also ship's stores and clothes and equipment. The motor and I companionably shared the galley. A bowl, toilet and medicine cabinet were installed in the smallest bathroom I'd ever seen. Aft of what I insisted on calling downstairs was a canopied cockpit with semi-enclosed wheelhouse.

The scheme to learn seamanship by doing it had other compensations. While outfitting, each hour was so full of fresh discoveries we had no time for apprehensions about the future. Collecting three months' supplies and finding places in which to put them occupied us so completely for a couple of days I'd almost forgotten we were going to sea. But the sinking feeling in the pit of my stomach caused by the skipper's announcement that it was time to sail was over almost as quickly as a tooth is extracted, for as the *Yakima* nosed into the ship canal I had to give all attention to my duties as mate when we passed through the Lake Washington canal locks. My excitement over that ordeal shut out all other thoughts.

Thus, to me it was a matter of some surprise to find ourselves suddenly upon salt water. The days of preparation and planning were over. There was something final in the opening of the great gate of the locks. We had gone to sea. Our self-taught seamanship did not go forward entirely without mishap but every lesson was cheap at the price. Getting lost in a fog when barely out of Seattle convinced us that a compass was more than a seagoing gadget that lent a nautical air to a boat. Ours didn't point north and we set about at once to work out a card of corrections.

Likewise our knowledge increased the night we sat on shore and strained our eyes in the breaking dawn to see if the *Yakima*, aground on a shelving reef, was going to slip off into deep water before she righted. The threat of losing our boat before we'd cruised 200 miles was an unforgettable demonstration in how suddenly a carefree voyage can change into disaster. Robert learned what a tidal range of from eight to twenty feet can uncover in the way of hidden rocks and I had a lesson in stowing which lasted through seven years. When the *Yakima* heeled over, everything in the boat except the motor and cookstove went adrift.

Two windbound days in harbor did not teach me patience but did give me some inkling of the inexorability of the sea. And an unwise crossing of the Gulf of Georgia, into which I prodded the skipper before a westerly had died down, convinced me that on a family-crewed voyage the mate must learn to handle the wheel even when great hissing combers are throwing a boat around. A two-man craft has no room for a fair-weather mate.

Our lessons were not all rigorous. Reasons behind ship's discipline dawned on us slowly. The sea, rather than the skipper, was the martinet and fulfillment of ship's duties not only smoothed routine but added to the comfort and happiness aboard. Keeping shipshape wasn't merely indulgence of a seagoing male's passion for order but a matter of always being ready for emergencies.

It paid other bonuses. With tasks done, we were free to enjoy the new life which absorbed us and were an ecstatic trio in the wheelhouse as we voyaged through a sunlit sea with great snow-capped mountains in the distance. We rode at anchor in quiet harbors and watched shadows lengthen as the sun slipped behind a peak and the peace and beauty of an evening on the "salt chuck" took possession. Waterfowl carried on their fussy little concerns and talked soft chit-chat. A seal might swim close to inspect us, and when a fish broke water the splash only blended with the twilight sounds.

We'd set out to see the inlet region, a spectacularly beautiful coast line lovelier, some maintained, than even the fiords of Norway. An ancient conflict between the sea and the mountains had provided a cruising paradise. For a thousand miles north of Puget Sound, the continental coast had once extended farther into the Pacific with an outer range of mountains, a deep valley cut by ancient rivers and an inner range of stupendous heights, when, before the last glacial period, the whole coast tilted seaward. The outer range became an archipelago extending through Southeastern Alaska. The great land valley is now the famous Inside Passage through which ships travel to Alaska, and the mainland range, partly submerged and partly victorious over the sea's invasion, has become a vast, intricate network of straits, channels, sounds, bays and arms. Former foothills are hidden reefs, higher peaks are islands, mountain shoulders are points and headlands. Steep-walled canyons of ancient rivers are long winding ribbons of salt water which penetrate to the very heart of a great range, and mountains now rise straight from salt water.

We'd known these geological facts, but there can be no intellectual approach to the stunning effect of one's first American fiord. As the *Yakima* made her way up the narrow, twisting reaches of Jervis Inlet into that great gash in the lofty mountains known as Princess Louisa, we were silenced. For a million years those mountains had stood far from the sea and then the sea had come among them. It carried us now beneath great peaks. It seemed that we looked straight up past unbroken forest mantles to glittering snowfields. We were on the sea, and we were in the mountains. And everywhere tiny streams crept out from beneath the snow, danced to the edges of the precipices and leaped out into the sea.

That night we anchored so close to a mountain we could have cast a dry fly on its base. That mountain lifted eighty-four hundred feet above the sea on which we lay. And that night we knew what we wanted. We wanted a boat large enough to live on, to work on, a craft that would be a real home afloat. We didn't know how we would get it, but the beauty of Princess Louisa had decided us.

It was mid-August when we turned south from the head of Knight Inlet, longest of the fiords and one of the most remote, and began a daylong run to where it joined the Pacific. Knight was a grand finale. Its peaks were higher and more precipitous and, set at the end of a long reach like a clear blue jewel, glittered our first glacier.

We couldn't have turned back without visiting Knight Inlet, and now that we had done so we weren't satisfied. We thought of the bigger inlets to the north, of higher mountains and greater glaciers. We had cruised for weeks and only scratched the surface. Now we must start homeward.

Our days, our weeks, our months had been crammed with living. There'd not been a moment in which we could not look out at beauty. We'd been afloat so long the sounds, smells and movement of the sea were a part of life. We'd anchored in lonely harbors and near homes of the dwellers in that amazing sea country. We'd moored at a float town, a village on the sea nestling at the foot of a mountain. We'd met fishermen. We'd watched that one-man logging crew, a handlogger, drop a 200-foot fir so cunningly it shot down a steep mountainside like a projectile and did not stop until it was a log in the sea. We'd begun to learn sea ways. We'd taken our craft through the Yucluetaws, one of the two great bottlenecks through which flows the tidal water necessary to serve a great complicated region.

In the Yucluetaws the magnitude and inexorability of this tidal movement builds to a climactic burst of power. Twice each lunar day the level of an elaborate network of straits, inlets, arms, bays and coves, down to the very last tiny indentation, rises and falls from eight to twenty feet. All the water for this great surge and ebb in that region must flow through a restricted twisting channel four miles long. The turn of the tide, when the current ceases to run in one direction and begins its sweep in the other, is known as slack, and is the only period in which the rapids are navigable. As the tide gathers force, its first low mutter grows into a sullen roar, and the surface of the water is no longer a smooth straight sweep but a broken angry passage. Huge whirlpools form. Masses of water, deflected by hidden ledges, break the surface in great upsurging boils an acre in extent. As the push of the tide increases, the roar intensifies. The channel is a welter of turbulence and confusion. Its threat is terrifying.

When at last the tidal law has been fulfilled to its last drop, the clamor begins to lessen and at last halts for a momentary peace before the mad surge begins in the opposite direction.

To me the Yucluetaws was as stirring as any symphonic poem. We spent a week just inside the entrance to the rapids, safely moored to a fisherman's float, and it was for me a week of emotional excitement. I'd wait for the buildup of the tide as expectantly as I ever waited for that moment when all the instruments of an orchestra blend and join in one great triumphant strain.

The summer had held many great moments. We were carrying home memories of mountains, of peace and contentment in quiet anchorages, of sparkling days, of the joy of waking to see sun reflected from the water on the white ceiling of the cabin. But we'd begun to talk about these things in retrospect. And that was sad. It was like talking over a party we hadn't wanted to leave.

And always there'd been booty days. My love of wresting booty from the country was a family joke and even Bobs teased me about my clam-digging grin. Clam beaches, crab flats, trout streams, salmon runs, rocky ledges where cod lingered and berry bushes ashore, each gave me a field day.

That booty meant so much to me was not due to my attitude toward food but to my sex. Women haven't come far since food and a comfortable cave were the main considerations in life and earth's bounty quickly stirs their racial memories. I'd noticed this often. A man may hunt or fish for love of the sport but the first question his wife asks is, "Did you get anything, darling?" When we'd hunted or fished with others I'd seen a lustful gleam in women's eyes as they brought in their trophies. The atavistic streak in women is very wide. Game, to them, means a replenishment of the larder.

I admitted all this readily.

"If I didn't have a primitive instinct, this outdoor game wouldn't be so real," I said. "And I'd have missed a lot of fun this summer."

"None of us missed any fun this summer," Robert said. "Best we've ever had."

His voice trailed off wistfully and we were back again on that mournful theme of farewell. We'd not thought of a way to get that larger boat, though we'd learned its requirements in comfort and safety. It was no longer a matter of how little we could manage with but of those factors we weren't willing to go without. Anything short of a home afloat in which we could carry on the job would be only a sorry makeshift. The novel would bring mid-winter royalties, but that check was already budgeted as the beginning of our savings, security for our future. It was high time we made investments.

"And perhaps some day they'll grow into a yacht," I said.

"When you and I are so old the smell of salt water makes us sneeze," Robert said. "We've seen a grand country. Let's forget it."

He steered in silence while I reviewed chats I'd had with bankers on the dazzling rewards of providence and foresight. Royalties from a best seller would give us the first opportunity to make real preparations for those later years.

"We've *got* to invest that money where it's safe!" I burst forth.

"Sure," Robert said. "We've got no right to fritter away or gamble a stake like that."

And then we looked at each other.

"Lo bailado nadie me lo quita," I said.

Long ago an old Spaniard had said this and had given us the translation. "That which has been danced no one can take from me." I'd thought we understood its wisdom and now suddenly I knew how little it had taught us. In mistaken frugality we were actually planning to be spendthrifts with the years.

"No one's ever lost a moment that's been lived or a memory that's been hoarded," I said. "Let's invest that money where it's really safe and buy a ship."

We invested more than money in the *Triton*.

We bought her in mid-winter when her former owner, who'd built her as his last and perfect craft, decided he couldn't afford her, and from the moment of ownership we regretted every day spent in San Francisco while Bobs finished the school year and I had a bout with surgery. Nurses, hospital bills and surgeon's fees are always painful, but these defrauded the *Triton*.

It was an enchanted summer. We visited favorite harbors and old friends and discovered new. We were voyaging, yet we were at home. Robert did his fiction stint in the morning. Bobs spent hours rowing in her own dinghy. I was something between mate, housewife and a carefree adventurer. We went for day's explorations up small rivers in a kicker-propelled dinghy. We fished. We berried. Bobs and I went swimming. The days weren't long enough. And the evenings, when all three lay on the foredeck to watch the colors of sunset fade and the twilight hush envelop our small world, were hours of delight.

When we finally turned south we did so with no regrets. All that coast line to the north and the Inside Passage to Alaska would be ours in future years. We were ready to rebuild the *Triton*. Like any remodeling plan, it had grown more elaborate. We'd spent the summer discarding and devising. Rebuilding was to be a major operation. Six feet added to the stern would give us a full fifty feet of boat, an afterdeck and a stateroom for Bobs. A deckhouse would afford lounging quarters and comfort while cruising. Below decks were a large main cabin, a bathroom with real bathtub, a convenient galley and our own stateroom and bathroom.

"No one could ask for a better seagoing home than that," I said.

The rebuilt *Triton* fulfilled our hopes. What had been merely lines on paper were now lounging, living and working quarters with lockers everywhere. We could stow supplies for a five months' cruise. We had a year-round home. Not since the wilderness cabin days had we plunged into home settling with such fervor.

Bobs spent hours getting her stateroom accoutered for the varied occupations of an eleven-year-old. Clothes rated lower than paints, crayons, charcoal, drawing pads, marine collections, odds and ends of tinfoil, modeling clay, books and cutting tools. I wondered where the new dog would sleep, until I saw his blanket spread at the foot of her berth.

Alaska was impossible that year and we lived a summer home existence. We even voyaged in a summer colony. Betty and Stewart White, whom we'd met two years before, had again put their fifty-footer, *Dawn*, into commission and the two boats cruised together. As both craft were crewless, our schedules tallied. The skippers worked in the morning. Afternoons were spent swimming, fishing, cruising or in land expeditions. While the men were at their fiction stint, Betty, Bobs and I engaged in seagoing women's affairs, and there was never a more spirited companion for any sort of affairs, sea or otherwise, than Betty White.

September sent us on our separate ways. The Whites departed for California after ordering a new boat to cruise Alaska the next summer. Alaska would be as new to them as to us and all looked forward to that convoy cruise.

For three years we had talked of the day when we would jump off for Alaska, talked until it didn't seem possible that any country could meet our anticipation. But we hadn't been in those northern waters a week before we knew we had come to a new and exciting cruising ground.

Southeastern Alaska is a robust, roistering, untamed land. The mountains rise to new heights and blaze with color in rock and foliage. Waterways are not an hour's but a day's cruise, and the prodigality of this sea country draws eager fingers across charts. Rivers, mountains, glaciers, reaches, island mazes, snug anchorages in coves and precarious holdings in glacier winds, all these fill days with adventure and loveliness.

Sharing the excitement of discovery with Betty and Stewart White only added to our breathless state. But after a few days we realized that Southeastern Alaska was a Gargantuan feast. We couldn't gulp it down in one summer and we decided to make a wide survey so that the next year we could narrow down our choices.

The cruise took every moment and every ounce of energy, and always was worth the cost. The Whites' new fifty-eight footer was crewed with engineer and cook, which put the *Triton* family crew at a disadvantage in keeping up with schedule. Our cruising fell into a regular pattern, one day to explore a river, the next day to reach another, and small boats departed immediately after breakfast for these daylong expeditions upstream. But nothing would have made us miss a river. They were too exciting, too varied and too lovely.

Such intensive sightseeing demanded system on the *Triton*. To be free at anchorage, we must do boat work when under way, and as we voyaged we cleaned ship, polished brass, attended to odd jobs, cooked and even laundered. Bobs' rating was changed from bo'sun to quartermaster.

We'd not expected boarding school to train a seaman, but the self-reliant twelve-year-old who returned to us could stand a trick at the wheel, take charge of her quarters and pinch-hit forward. I began to understand the importance English people attach to their public school system. It doesn't make adults of children but it does encourage them to be persons. Our educational experiment had worked out happily. Bobs' progress in studies had not been spectacular, but she was well started on the job of growing into a real woman. And she loved the school.

Our two months in Alaska were crammed. We saw its cities and explored its rivers. We visited its glaciers and watched great bergs, the size of office buildings, break from the face and take to sea. We skirted the three big islands on which the brown bears live and watched the great grizzlies fish for salmon. We marveled at streams where trout lay so densely packed the bottom of the stream was darkly mottled. We traveled rivers filled with salmon fighting their way to the spawning ground. We saw Alaska bathed in sunlight and ravishing in color, and we did not try to find words to express the bold grandeur of its snow-capped mountains. We saw Alaska in rain and discovered that it is as prodigal with rainfall as with all other things. We marked off our favorite regions and knew which rivers we would always visit and which great stretches of sea-invaded ranges we must always see.

Discovery of Southeastern Alaska extended the *Triton's* radius and the northern thrust became the exciting cruise of the year. Never again did we cover quite so much territory in a season, but we saw the country more intensively.

The knowledge that this two months' adventure awaited us didn't detract from our normal life afloat. Each season had its own particular flavor, was spent in a different region and in different activities. Spring overhaul was a time of anticipation. There was always a rush to get the *Triton* groomed and ready for Easter holidays, when Bobs brought friends aboard. In September after Bobs had departed for school, Robert and I turned the bow of the *Triton* toward our fall cruising grounds and took up our regular home life again. We weren't summer people. We were dwellers in a sea country.

Southeastern Alaska is only the vestibule to the real Alaska, and Alaskans are firm on this matter. A glance at the map will show Southeastern Alaska to be a long tail hanging from a vast land. It is a region of magnificent mountains, breath-taking beauty and startling contrasts, for glaciers neighbor with growth that is tropical in luxuriance, but this lovely corridor is not the land of the midnight sun. Nor is it to be confused with "out to the westward," the Alaskans' term for the long peninsula extending to the Aleutian Islands.

"Out to the westward" were higher mountains, larger glaciers and waters famous in whaling and sealing history. But the six-hundred-mile open crossing of the Gulf of Alaska was not possible for our family crew. We could only envy every boat we saw outfitting for that cruise.

We had become conscious of how little of the real Alaska we had penetrated and this awareness proved we needed new waters across our bows. For years we had been running the same old courses and repeating the same experiences. Yet in a boat which did not permit crew's quarters we couldn't extend our radius.

A home afloat must be ever moving. We did not think this out. It was a conviction that grew slowly within us. Perhaps the fact that Bobs would matriculate in June and must return to the United States to continue her education may have increased our awareness that once again we had outgrown a home. A boat had fitted prep school days and our own explorations of an exciting sea country. Now it failed to meet our needs.

It was a shock to us to admit this. But we could not deny its truth. Cutting free must always bring regret and even sorrow, but remaining past the moment of farewell brings disillusionment. Memories are too precious to be despoiled, and if one must leave a ship, a home or a woman, leave should be taken while one is still in love.

The *Triton* had never seemed more desirable or more lovely than the day when we stood on a yacht club pier and watched her disappear down the fairway. The bill of sale declared that she now belonged to another but we knew she was ours and always would be. Nothing could rob us of the *Triton*, nor of those seven years.

Outfall: The Border Country

Up Revillagigedo Channel the scenery is more like that of
the Scotch lakes, broad expanses of water walled by forest
ridges and mountains that in certain lights show a glow like
blooming heather on their sides.

Eliza Scidmore

EIGHT

A Canoe Voyage into the Tongas Country

by Sheldon Jackson

I had long wanted to make a visit to the missions of the Methodist and Episcopal Churches at Fort Simpson and Metlahkatlah, and inspect their plans and methods of labor. The latter of these missions has been in operation twenty years, and sufficient time has elapsed to test the efficiency of their methods. Besides, these missions were the forerunner of our own work in Alaska. Unable to visit them in any other way, I concluded, during my visit to Alaska in 1879, to make the trip in a canoe. Just at that time a large one came in from the Chilcat country, loaded with furs and bound for Fort Simpson. As a portion of the crew were Christian Indians from Fort Simpson, there was no difficulty in arranging a passage. Besides the six Christian Indians, there were twelve wild Chilcat savages, headed by two chiefs, one of whom was a medicine-man or shaman.

The canoe was about thirty-five feet long, five wide, and three deep. A comfortable seat was allotted me in the centre, with my blanket and provisions within easy reach. On the 11th of August we left Fort Wrangell for Fort Simpson and Metlahkatlah, B.C. The day wore on with the monotonous dip of the paddles. Rounding a cape, they were able to hoist two sails, and have their assistance for a short distance.

Late in the afternoon we passed an abandoned Stickeen village. A number of the ancient *totem* poles were still standing, surmounted by grotesque images, and containing the bones and ashes of the former inhabitants. Many had fallen and are rotting amid the dense undergrowth of bushes and ferns. Some of the corner-posts of their large houses were still standing, resting upon the top of which are immense beams, some of them three feet through and from forty to sixty feet long.

Without an inhabitant, the coarse croaking of the raven alone broke in upon the stillness and desolation of the scene. The Indians, resting upon their paddles, gazed intently at the ruins as we floated by with the tide. What thoughts were passing through their minds I had no means of knowing. Perhaps the savage Chilcats looked upon the scene with superstitious dread and awe, while to the Christian Tsimpseans it brought joy and gratitude as they more fully realized that the heathen darkness of the past had been changed to light and hope.

Frequently along the way the Chilcat Indians would break out into singing one of their national airs, to cheer the rowers. This would challenge the Christian Indians, who would follow with a number of the precious hymns of Bliss and Sankey. One evening, after a large number of these had been sung, the old Chilcat and shaman inquired, "Who is this Jesus you sing about?" Then the Tsimpsean Indians gladly preached Jesus unto him.

These Christian Indians carry their religion with them wherever they go. They were now returning from a voyage of over a thousand miles. They had been on the way for weeks. But under no circumstances would they travel on the Sabbath. Upon one occasion they were nearly out of food, and their heathen companions urged them to continue the voyage, that they might reach an Indian village and procure supplies. The heathen said, "We are hungry, and you are no friends of ours if you do not go where we can get something to eat." But neither tide, wind, nor hunger could induce them to travel on the Lord's day. One of them afterward said, in a meeting of his own people, that his heart was often sad upon the trip because he did not know more of the language of the people they were visiting, and could not tell them more about Jesus.

It is the universal testimony of the whites, both friends and foes of the missions, that the Christian Indians of Metlahkatlah, Fort Simpson, and Fort Wrangell are strict in the observance of the Sabbath.

I was much interested in my Chilcat companions, and, like the Christian Indians, deplored that I could not more fully communicate with them. However, after we reached Fort Simpson, where an interpreter could be had, they came and sought a council. These people occupy the country at the head of Lynn Channel, and were known to the Hudson Bay Fur Company, at an early day, as the Nehaunees. They are a bold, warlike, and enterprising people. They are also noted traders, being the middle-men between the interior tribes and the American merchants on the coast. They number about two thousand.

I also had a council with some Hydahs. We camped one night on their island. They re-echoed the universal desire of the people along this coast for schools, and I promised to bring their case also before the board.

At Fort Simpson I was visited by a delegation of Tongas, who had the same request to make for help. I could only promise to try and interest the Church in their behalf. The Indians think that the whites have some great secret about the future state of the soul, which they wish to learn. They are in a condition of expectancy which would cause them warmly to welcome Christian teachers. But if this season is permitted by the Church to pass away unimproved, who can say that it will not be followed by greater hardness of heart and more determined heathenism?

About six p.m. the canoe was run upon the beach, and an hour spent in supper, after which they paddled until ten o'clock, when, finding an opening in the rock-bound coast, we put ashore, spread our blankets upon the sand, and were soon sound asleep. At three a.m. we were roused and were soon under way, without any breakfast. This, however, did not matter much, as my stock of provisions consisted of ship biscuit for dinner. The Indians upon the trip only averaged one meal the twenty-four hours.

During the morning, passing the mouth of a shallow mountain stream, the canoe was anchored for a few minutes, while poles and paddles clubbed to death some thirty salmon, averaging twenty-five pounds each in weight. These were thrown into the canoe and taken along.

At noon they put ashore for their first meal that day. Fires were made under shelter of a great rock. The fish, cleaned and hung upon sticks, were soon broiling before the fire. After dinner all hands took a nap upon the beach. At three p.m. we were again under way. When night came, finding no suitable landing-place, the Indians paddled on until two o'clock next morning, having made a day's work of twenty-three hours. At two a.m., finding a sheltered bay, we ran ashore. As it was raining hard, we spread our blankets as best we could, under sheltering rocks or projecting roots of the great pines.

At six o'clock, rising from an uncomfortable sleep, we embarked and paddled until nine, when, reaching the cabin of Mr. Morrison, at Tongas Narrows, we went ashore for breakfast. Mr. Morrison has a fine vegetable garden, and is also engaged in salmon fisheries. At this point I secured two fine specimens of stone axes.

In an hour we were again under way, the Indians working hard at the paddles until the middle of the afternoon, when we ran ashore upon a rocky point for a short rest and sleep, the sea being very rough.

In an hour and a half we were again on our journey. Toward evening we passed Cape Fox and boldly launched out to cross an arm of the sea, and once out it was as dangerous to turn back as to go forward. The night was dark, the waves rolling high, and the storm upon us. One Indian stood upon the prow of the canoe watching the waves and giving orders. Every man was at his place, and the stroke of the paddles kept time with the measured song of the leader, causing the canoe to mount each wave with two strokes; then, with a click, each paddle would, at the same instant, strike the side of the canoe and remain motionless, gathering strength for the next wave. As the billows struck the canoe it quivered from stem to stern.

It was a long, tedious night, as in the rain and fog and darkness we tossed in a frail canoe upon the waters, but daylight found us near Fort Tongas.

This is an Indian village and an abandoned military post. From the water there seemed to be a whole forest of crest or *totem* poles. Many of them are from sixty to seventy-five feet high, and carved from top to bottom with a succession of figures representing the eagle, wolf, bear, frog, whale, and other animals. The military post was established in 1867 and abandoned in 1877. The buildings are still standing. The chief has repeatedly, in a most earnest and urgent manner, asked for a teacher for his people before, through the combined effect of vice and whiskey, they become extinct.

The wind had been against us all the way from Fort Wrangell. It had rained more or less each day that we had been out, and the storm had continued to increase in violence. Some of the Indians being so exhausted by the labors of the past night that they dropped asleep at their paddles, it was thought best to go ashore and get some rest. On shore we tried to start a fire, but the driving rain soon extinguished it. Taking my regulation meal of salmon and hard-tack, I spread my blankets under a big log and tried to sleep. The beating storm soon saturated the blankets, and I awoke to find the water running down my back. Rising, I paced up and down the beach until the Indians were ready to move on. After a rest of two hours, seeing no signs of a lull in the storm, we re-embarked determined, if possible, to make Fort Simpson.

Getting out of the shelter of the island into Dixon's Inlet, we found the wind in our favor. Hoisting both sails, we drove through the waves at a slashing rate, the corner of the sails dipping into the water, and occasionally the waves running over the side into the canoe. This was fun for the Indians, who would again and again exclaim, as our masts bent under the sails, "Beat steamboat! Beat steamboat!" Cold, wet, and hungry, that afternoon we ran into the harbor at Fort Simpson, and shortly after were receiving a warm welcome at Rev. Thomas Crosby's mission of the Methodist Church of Canada.

NINE

Daughter of the Coast

by Barrett Willoughby

She brought the *Golden Hind* back on its course.

She should, of course, turn and go back home where she had left her house guest, Eve Galliard, fast asleep. But something—was it the hope of coming upon the offending *Who Cares* in distress!— impelled her to go on. She was running close to shore now, past boulders hung with brown and gold rockweed; past pendant- boughed hemlocks; silver-blue spruce. The channel swung ahead, an enticing silver lane in the warm light. Distant mountains below their snows were blue as larkspur, soft as plush. Mist hung low in the valleys. She had been aware of all this before, yet of a sudden it seemed to have taken on a new glamour.

In a flash of exuberance she leaned from the door of the pilot- house and called a greeting to an eagle sunning itself on a high tree- top.

The great bird somersaulted from its perch and headed into the wind with slow beats of its powerful wings. Watching its easy flight gave Dian a fine feeling of freedom. She, too, was going to be glori- ously free during these two weeks of Alaskan summer that were hers. After that she would be quite content to go back to the States, marry Alan, and make his charming, easeful life her own.

Two weeks... fourteen days.... The time, all at once, seemed very short, very precious. There were so many beloved places and things to which she must say good-bye. The *Golden Hind*, for instance, named after the regal privateer of Sir Francis Drake. True, after she was married, Alan would get her a small motor yacht if she wanted one; but no other craft, however splendid, could take the place in her heart occupied by this little cream-colored cruiser which had been her vacation delight ever since she was eighteen.

With a swift poignancy compounded of affection and farewell her mind embraced everything about the *Golden Hind*, even the old phonograph whose music had made sunset waters so enchanting during bygone summers. This morning the ripple at the prow and the steady, muffled throb of the engine made melody enough for her ears. She ran her supple hands over the wheel to feel again that sense of restrained power that always came to her from the contact.

A love of keels and salt-water things had been Dian Turlon's all her twenty-four years; at least, ever since her baby feet had taken their first wavering steps along the deck of the *Star of Alaska*. Her mother's father, the tawny-bearded old Viking, Nils Nilsson, was master of that lofty-sparred square-rigger which each spring led the Alaska Packers' salmon fleet out through the Golden Gate. Dian would never forget those trips of her childhood—the bark, gallant and romantic: her stately spread of canvas, her gleaming, holystoned deck, the proud lift of her figurehead, the Golden Flying Lady, as she bore away into the north Pacific, her cavernous hold filled with cannery supplies and crews for the far-flung fishing grounds of Bering Sea.

Dian's father, keen young Irishman, was superintendent then for the Packers' Cannery at the mouth of the Karluk River, the greatest salmon stream in the world. Each season he took his family with him on the *Star*'s April sailing out of San Francisco—her mother, her little brother Ivor, and herself. And in September when the salmon run was over, he brought them back to the States again with his crew.

After he left the Packers, he became an independent canner in southeastern Alaska. Some ten years ago he had built the big Turlon home in Ketchikan where his family lived during the summers and occasionally during a winter. He had also bought the *Star of Alaska*, the fastest packet in the white-winged salmon fleet.

His friends laughed at him for that, because steam and gasoline had already sounded the knell of sailing ships. But her father was always a law unto himself, Dian recalled proudly. There was something swift and strong in him that attained his ends. That was why everyone called him 'Eagle' Turlon, instead of his given name, Patrick. At any rate, the *Star of Alaska* was at this moment lying at the dock of the big Turlon cannery at Sunny Cove, some fifty miles down the coast from Ketchikan. This spring, as always, it had transported his cannery crew and supplies from Seattle.

Only a man as rich as her father could afford such a gesture; for he kept the great ship waiting at Sunny Cove until the season's pack was ready to be taken South in the autumn. That was the way it had waited in those early and more leisurely days when Eagle Turlon was a 'high man' for the Packers, and Dian's mother was alive.

She knew why he kept the old bark in commission. It was aboard the *Star* that he had met and instantly fallen in love with the daughter of Nils Nilsson. The skipper had raved like a madman when he found that Irish Eagle Turlon had run off with his Swedish Elna and married her at the nearest Russian mission at the height of the salmon run! Dian smiled to herself recalling her father's way of bellowing at her: " 'Tis the combination of 'harp' and 'ski jumper' in you, my girl, that makes you so damned disturbing!"

Certainly he would disapprove of her now if he knew she had come back to Ketchikan in his absence. Though she adored him, she felt a keen satisfaction touched with a certain humor, as she thought of him well on his way to Siberia seeking to extend his packing operations to that distant coast.

It was because of the uncertainty of the run in Alaska, a fact which her father never admitted outside his family, that he had sold three of his canneries. He retained only Sunny Cove, his pride. Sunny Cove, the largest, most modern plant in southeastern Alaska, with its twelve great salmon traps, its fleet of cannery tugs and seine-boats. This he was holding for eighteen-year-old Ivor whom he had bullied into studying ichthyology at the University of Washington. Ivor, who wanted to be a musician!

Ironically, Dian was the one who loved everything connected with the fish run. But women had no place in this fascinating game that had held her father in thrall for more than thirty-five years. Dian had been able to do little more than snatch at that romance which endures wherever sturdy bronzed men garner the world's food from the sea.

Romance.... For some reason the thought brought a vision of the slim, dark young man looking at her from the pilot-house of the seiner, *Who Cares*. Yet he hadn't quite the look of a fisherman. Who was he? Where had he gone? She smiled to herself, remembering the rope trailing precariously in his wake; and her gaze swung, searching the sun-bright empty waters ahead.

Her attention was arrested by one of the Turlon fish traps across a small bay that opened to her left. It lay on the water off Kemerlee Head in readiness for the legal opening of the fishing season a week hence. She put her wheel over and headed for it. Abreast the floating trap she shut off her engine and drifted along the criss-cross pattern of logs, large as the foundation of an office building. At one end was a tiny shack with a small window in each wall through which a man might watch the approach of strange craft or shoot at trespassers. Here, during the run, a watchman would live to protect the catch from depredations of fish pirates.

Floating traps had always interested Dian more than the larger pile-driven kind used on the open coast. This Kemerlee Head floater was anchored some distance from the shore. Its heavy timbers held suspended the labyrinth of webbing that formed the 'pot,' the 'heart,' the 'spiller,' net-enclosed compartments that glimmered fathoms down in the clear depths. About it all was the cool, clean tang of salt water against spruce wood.

It was peaceful here in the sun; a tranquil inlet surrounded by forested hills and blue mountains crowned with dimming snows. Quiet, too, except for the lapping of water against the logs. Yet in the very hush there was a strange expectancy. The great trap swung above its anchors... waiting. Dian thought of the hundreds of like devices placed at every strategic point, in every deep-cut fiord of southeastern Alaska... each one waiting for that mighty silver host now cleaving northward through the green coastal waters.

She hoped fervently that the run would be good this year and that it would begin before she had to return to the States. "Maybe this will help—" she said to herself; and half in play, half in earnest, she spread wide her arms, lifted her face, and with eyes closed chanted in the manner of an Indian supplicating the Alaskan Mother of All Salmon:

"O Fog Woman! Call your North-born children home!"

As Dian speeded up her engine to continue her morning run, she regretted that she hadn't had time to provision the larder on the *Golden Hind*. She might then have cruised down as far as Green Waters, caught a few trout, and cooked one of her old-time breakfasts aboard. But no, she remembered suddenly: Eve Galliard—her self-invited guest—back home and probably awake now. Silken, lazy, perfumed Eve. "She no more belongs here in Alaska than I belong in Timbuctoo!" thought Dian, her eyes moving over the serene, virgin landscape.

But a guest is a guest, and thoughts of the waiting Eve, coupled with a vision of old Suey Woo padding about the big kitchen preparing a delectable breakfast, finally made Dian swing her cruiser back on the return course.

When she came in sight of the floating trap again, she espied a boat made fast to the frame. Through the binoculars the craft leaped close. She recognized it with a triumphant little grin—the insolent *Who Cares*, out of commission with that rope wound round its propeller!

In a manner that reflected her father's own dashing way with a cruiser, she speeded toward the moored boat.

She swung in close and slowed down a few yards from the seiner. So far as she could see there was no one aboard. Then, as the *Golden Hind* came to a stop, she was startled to observe a head shoot up from the water off the stern of the *Who Cares*. Thick black hair dripped down over nose and eyes. Tight shut teeth gripped a villainous-looking knife in a way she had never thought to see outside the illustrations in a pirate book. A couple of strong strokes, and the owner of the head was treading water beside a trap timber. He drove the knife into the log with a quick motion that lifted his body, and Dian saw the smoothly muscular back of an athlete, bare wet arms and shoulders glistening in the sun, bronzed neck and forearms. High up on the biceps of his right arm was tattooed a small flying gull.

Apparently he had not heard the muffled approach of the *Golden Hind*, for he made a movement to clamber up on the frame of the trap.

"Hello!" Dian sang out hastily.

He tossed his head to throw the hair back from his face, and, keeping one arm over the log, turned to regard her from a pair of cool, deliberate, deep-blue eyes.

"Hello!" he responded. There was both power and mockery in the curve of his lips, and, though Dian could detect no welcoming note in his voice, she liked its deep masculine quality. "Where did you come from?"

"Oh, I just dropped in for a moment. I thought you might be in need of a tow."

"A tow?" His air of interrogation was perfect. From his lowly position he flashed her an answering smile that showed firm white teeth. "No. Thank you very much." A faint, provocative amusement hid behind his words. "I wasn't expecting company and—well, you find me just following the quaint old Alaskan custom of taking a morning dip."

Dian was swept with the stinging warmth of embarrassment. For a second he convinced her that she had, in truth, blundered upon just that occasion. Then, nettled by the man's poise even while she admired it, she looked at him with a level, appraising glance she had inherited from Eagle Turlon. Meaningly her eyes traveled from face to the thickened propeller glimmering under the stern of the *Who Cares*, and back again. A moment later she raised her chin with a low, rippling laugh of derision.

"Another quaint old Alaskan custom, I suppose—this gripping a hunting-knife in your teeth as you perform your ablutions. What do you do with it?" she asked with calculated sweetness. "Use it instead of soap?"

Without giving him a chance to answer, she started her engine and in her most spectacular manner swung the *Golden Hind* on its homeward course.

As she left the trap behind, she found that the encounter had set her heart beating faster. There was something distinctly challenging about that dark young man. She knew now he was no inexperienced boatman. He had merely been careless, and in his masculine pride had not wanted her to know it. He was the kind who would have paddled the *Who Cares* to Ketchikan with his hands, if possible, rather than have a woman tow him in.

She didn't need to look back now to know that he was diving off the trap and coming up under the stern of his craft to cut the rope free.... Only an excellent swimmer could do that in these cold Northern fiords.... A wet, glistening figure flashing through the sunlight into the still, green water.... Strong.... Beautiful, too. Smooth-skinned, glowing with health. And that pale-blue flying gull on the point of his shoulder— something suggestive of travel in that; of far-away places...

Men were mysterious, glamorous creatures.

Of a sudden the waterways, mountains, the cloud-piled azure sky, the whole Northern world, seemed inexplicably sunny and lyrical. She was aware that she was very young, buoyant, filled with the joy of life. Impulsively she lifted her face and raised one hand high as if to a benign and smiling friend. Then in a voice soft with a wonder and sincerity she said:

"Thank you, God!"

TEN

On the Way to Knudson Cove

by Edward A. Lawrence

While having breakfast, I happened to glance out of the window across the room. On the opposite beach, also seemingly inverted in the narrow sheet of sky-bright water, stood a doe. Her long ears swiveled inquiringly. The half-lifted foreleg clearly expressed indecision. She appeared to be taken aback by the two boats.

"Pop," I quivered, "there's a deer on the beach!"

He leaned over and peered out the window. He began breathing asthmatically. His eyes lit up like an old eagle's.

"Where's your gun," he whispered with great fierceness, "—on the boat?"

"Why, Pop," I chided, "isn't there a season on deer? And besides, that's a doe." I think I must have looked at Pop askance.

He grinned sheepishly. The wild light died away in his eyes. His breathing became less hoarse. "Yeah, I plum' forgot. I be dogged if I didn't. And, besides," he quickly added, "she sure 'nough is a doe, ain't she?"

He poured the saucer full of coffee. "Yeah...Yeah," he muttered absently, and blew.

This was the little black-tailed Sitkan deer, the only true deer indigenous to Alaska, and found only in the southeastern islands and along a thin strip of mainland coast. Not so large as the Virginian white-tailed or the Western mule deer, yet they are finely proportioned, dainty—and, so help me, delicious.

Pop studied her dispassionately. He reminded me of a stockman considering a baby beef.

"She figures somethin's wrong," he said. "Look at her ears goin' ever' which way."

Her smooth, tawny coat shone in the soft morning light. She twitched her tail, and took a hesitant step. Then, abruptly, with a startled look over her shoulder, she turned and bounded past the old cabin into the green, doubtful sanctuary of the forest.

"Lordy," Pop sighed, "such a life they lead, what with the wolves and all!"

"Yeah," I responded. I asked him if there were many wolves on Gravina.

"Lousy with 'em," he replied, succinctly. "But they're on all the islands, and actu'lly seem to be increasin'. You might get a crack at one this summer. There's a forty-dollar bounty waitin' if you do."

The sun had made a quarter of its long circling mid-summer orbit before we were ready to pull the skiff in and load up. A fine day seemed in prospect. The ragged reach of unclouded sky above the cove had that fathomless serenity, that utterly clean and inimitable blueness found only in the skies of northern latitudes; a westerly wind billowed the treetops; the channel water beyond the cove opening broke and glittered. We headed out.

Upon emerging from the passageway, I saw a high, dark object standing up from the water about a halfmile ahead. It looked somewhat like a black lateen sail, and it lolled about in the waves ominously. Pop saw it too, and pointed. And, suddenly I knew what it was—the dorsal fin of a killer whale.

The killer whale, strange as it may seem, is a member of the dolphin family. Nevertheless, he is the largest and most ferocious known carnivore that inhabits our planet. He is the original unsavory character. Gregarious, they generally travel in large and rapacious packs, or pods. Walruses, sharks, and all other whales give them a wide berth. The sea lion, the seal, and the salmon flee them in terror. It has even been established that they have knocked small boats to smithereens, doubtlessly under the impression that they were nourishing. They range in length from eighteen to thirty feet; they are mammalian and crafty; the teeth, eleven to twelve on the sides of each jaw, conical and recurved, constitute a terrible weapon. The proper procedure to follow when these creatures appear is quite simple: leave them alone.

As we cleared the entrance, the tall fin sank slowly into the water, and I saw it no more.

Since we had to stop off at an oil dock on the way to the pass, we headed for the lower point of Pennock. There were many boats moving about, which is always the case during a stretch of good weather. A gray Coast Guard cutter, outbound, bored down Tongass Narrows at full throttle. A halibuter, her decks almost awash, crossed our bow in the opposite direction. Over toward Annette Island, a troller, poles out, seemed almost motionless. The island itself arose abruptly from the water into lofty, snow-seamed peaks that today were clearly visible. This is the island on which the town of Metlakatla is located, an all-Indian village belonging to the Tsimpsheans, formerly of British Columbia. They were brought here in 1887 by Father William Duncan, an almost legendary missionary who believed in putting a vision to work.

The oil docks were scenes of much activity, as they always are at this time of year. Small boats, however, receive the same courteous consideration as do the small ships. Five black hoses twisted across the float. Each of these bore one of five labels: gasoline, diesel oil, kerosene, stove oil, and water. We took ours in bulk, rather than draft, several five-gallon cans of gas and kerosene, and a few quarts of lubricating oil.

After leaving the oil dock, we rolled up the channel in the overlapping wakes of the fishing flotilla. Boating weather is also flying weather, and the planes were out in force. They rose thunderously from the channel, trailing iridescent streamers of mist; they landed in long, whistling glides; they circled overhead. Many types of aircraft participated in these maneuvers before and above the town. Some were the familiar light planes, pontooned, such as are seen wherever you are. These, as well as the heavier amphibious machines, are available for charter. They all are principally employed in transporting passengers between Ketchikan and other Alaskan seabound towns, and in carrying the mail. Perhaps their most spectacular use is in conveying hunters and trout fishermen to the remote mountain lakes of the islands and the mainland. In fact, for a party with but a limited amount of time at their disposal, it is a—well—practical way to get to the good cutthroat, moose, grizzly and mountain goat grounds.

The cold storage plants at this season are quite the busiest places in town. Halibuters, trollers and packers cluster about the unloading docks; and the icing spouts roar day long. Traffic lessened as we continued up the narrowing channel; and before long we found ourselves alone at the neck of a watery funnel that widened some ten miles ahead to Vallenar Point on the left, the northern extremity of Gravina, and Point Higgins on the opposite, the Revillagigedo, shore. A few miles up the funnel we passed on our right Ward Cove, a deeply indented and alluring bay, and Refuge Cove, dotted with rocky, evergreen islets.

Presently, beyond and to the left of the funnel mouth, there revolved into view one of the most enchanting sights I have ever known: Guard Islands. Standing out there where wilderness sea roads meet, at the confluence of Clarence Strait, Behm Canal, and Tongass Narrows, these two grassy island gems, with on the larger a cluster of white buildings dominated by a tall, square tower and balanced by a group of conifers, always seemed to me rather unreal; to be a mirage of the fancy merely; and if I closed my eyes and opened them, the islands would be gone and there would be nothing there at all but the shining or somber sea. And yet, the purpose to which one of these is put seems a far cry from such a fantasy. Here the Coast Guard maintains a station, to service the light and to sound the dismalest diaphone that ever smote upon a mariner's ears.

Reaching out toward Guard Islands from Vallenar Point are several small islets. Trees crowd the first one of these, and make of the second an evergreen coronet. The others, excepting the outermost, when not awash on the higher tides, are barren, brown and draped with kelp, visible vertebrae of a subterranean backbone. The extreme islet of this chain is called Vallenar Rock. Between Guard Islands and Vallenar Rock the tides seethe and clash. Back of the islets lies Vallenar Bay; and beyond, miles away to the westward, stream the mountains of Prince of Wales.

As we continued up the Narrows, Cleveland Peninsula, an extension of the mainland, rose slowly against the sky, dead ahead. Clarence Strait washes one side, and Behm Canal the other. The cape, or point, is named Caamano.

We were almost abeam Point Higgins before the islands of Clover Passage began to unreel on our right. Behm Canal, which girdles Revillagigedo Island, is about five miles wide at this western end, from Point Higgins to Point Caamano. Clover Passage itself lies between Revillagigedo and a number of islands grouped in the canal. These, in the order of their appearance, were the southernmost of the Tatoosh Island group; then, in quick succession, Betton, the largest of any other; Pup, a satellite of Betton; and farther down, Clover Island. These, and others, shall be examined more carefully as they are later approached.

Distance does indeed lend enchantment.

Prince of Wales! Helm Bay! Caamano! How vivid and varied are the recollections I have of these places as seen from afar in so many perspectives of time and place and in all the changing weathers. These are the cherished and memoried features, which, I now know, a closer scrutiny could not possibly improve. Prince of Wales is to me simply what could be accomplished on canvas by a few strokes of the brush; this long rambling, sea-born island is but a far-off flash of sun-struck snows or a misty never-ever land; it is a headland of the sea into the flank of Cleveland Peninsula; Helm Bay is a portal to faeryland, a smoky blue mirage, and to me has somehow represented ideally that which is so illusively magical in this almost unbelievable land.

Looking up the pass, I saw no sign of any human habitation. It stirred me to think that I could see it as did Vancouver, well over a century ago. How generally unchanged it is may be illustrated by the fact that the great navigator had made a lithograph of a certain tall and monumental shaft of rock rising from a sand shoal in the opposite, or eastern end, of Behm Canal. This he named New Eddystone Rock, after a similar outcropping in an English harbor. A modern photograph of this rock compared with the original drawing shows but one difference: the few trees at the base of it are somewhat larger now than then.

We passed two small, open bays on our right, and a rugged projection of the shore, named Survey Point; then, a bit farther along, two hand trollers in small white boats, one cabined, one open, fishing close inshore. We waved and they waved. Beyond a second point, down close to the water in the curve of a bight, appeared two houses. In front of them a red troller rode at anchor.

Located in about the center of the pass stood a tiny tree-spired isle with a white marker containing a flashing light. Later, it would be referred to, not so simply, as "The Little Island with the Light." Now shortly after the turn of the tide, a sloping rock ridge could be seen making out toward Clover Island, a short distance beyond.

After passing the homesteads, we continued alongside a vertical rock wall; and presently came to the white, spindle-shaped object—"the Barrel," we called it—on a post over an underwater pinnacle, precisely where a boat would normally pass as it made the turn into Knudson Cove.

Having in more recent years acquired much prominence as a base anchorage and as a point of departure for sport fishing in Clover Passage, Knudson Cove on this twelfth day of June, 1946, was comparatively unknown to any but the commercial fishermen and the old-timers of Ketchikan and vicinity. Mountain Point was then the grounds for such sport fishing as obtained in those unenlightened and toilsome days.

The cove, formed somewhat like a misshapen 'V', is approximately a half-mile deep and about the same distance across the mouth. It is fair enough anchorage for most of the year, as it is rather well protected from the rampaging southeaster. There is no protection, however, from the north winds; but these are never severe except in the winter, and even then, but for rare and notable instances, are more of a nuisance than a menace. On a grassy point to my right stood a tiny, weathered cabin of hand-wrought cedar shakes, the original homestead, built by Knudson himself. It seemed a fitting memorial. A few houses, of recent and more formalized construction, appeared on the perimeter of the cove. Near the fork of the 'V' a pile-legged pier extended out to an attached float, the work of the Forest Service. And down on our right, near the mouth of a stream, swung into view the attractive little white home of Lawrence Carson.

We headed for a stretch of empty beach between this home and a narrow muskeg creek. To the right of our proposed campsite lay a beached wanigan, or float house, that belonged to someone in Ketchikan, and which remained empty and unused all summer long.

I had decided upon the cove as a base for several reasons. It was a protected anchorage, for one; and for another, a spur road led from the pier up to the highway into Ketchikan, sixteen miles away. An antique bus—the Ketchikan stage— made two round trips each day from town to the end of the road, a short distance beyond the cove; and an oil truck came out once a week—all of which really simplified the supply problem. I had also made arrangements with a friend, Arthur Smith, who owned a small panel truck, to take our catch into town each day. Art and his family, while working on their homestead, lived in a trailer near the end of the highway. Smith had succumbed to the boat virus, and he also contemplated fishing the pass.

Our keels grated on a black shale beach; the tapering shadows of the forest all about us; and as we cut the motors, a familiar silence again marched down and hummed pleasantly in our ears. While Pop watched the boats against the outgoing tide, I lugged our stores up to the trees. This had nearly been accomplished when I saw a man walking along the beach in our direction. He was slightly taller than the average, slender, wore crumpled hip-boots, a foul-weather jacket, and a black rain hat.

"Hello, there," he grinned. "Looking for a place to pitch your tent?"

Pop said howdy, and how was the fishing, and—to me —that this was "Kit" Carson. I introduced myself. Although I had never met him, Kit was really no stranger to me. I had read his pieces in *The Alaska Sportsman*, and had heard his name mentioned quite often. He epitomized the present-day Alaskan: well-informed, friendly, tolerant, self-reliant, a man of outstanding character and many parts.

"You came to a good place," he said. "You'll have a lot of fun. Some years the fishing is fairly good; some years it isn't. So far, it isn't. But you'll like it here in the cove."

He showed us where to pitch the tent, a level, gravelly place under the great trees, enclosed by a low plank wall, obviously an old tent site.

"An old Indian used to camp here," he said. "But he hasn't been out for a couple of years: I hear he's not well. That's his smokehouse beside the creek. This muskeg water, incidentally, is good to drink. Here, let me help you with that tent. . . ."

A Great River North: III

Inside Passage

by V.A. Eberhart

Sport? Sure, it's sport. The greatest sport on earth.

No, let's change that, to the greatest sport in the world, for the absence of earth makes it what it is. I still get as hefty a wallop out of landing a rampaging old king salmon as I did out of my first one, more than thirty years ago. That's the trouble. A man goes crazy when he gets one of those fighting fools on his line. Some of us never get over it.

Trolling for king and coho salmon in Alaska is called commercial fishing. Really, it is an excuse for a sport fisherman to forsake family, fireside and full-time employment to do the thing he enjoys most. With some, the joy fades fast when they start playing for keeps. I've seen some of the same boats make the run from Seattle to Ketchikan year after year, but each year with a different skipper, a new sucker. This particular year, I had two of them hung on my neck.

The old-timers usually leave Seattle late in March or early in April. I had decided, however, to leave in February for a little early fishing in March. The older I get, the less sense I seem to have in such matters.

It's a stormy time to run without the insurance of a partner boat—someone close in case of trouble. My wife soon took care of that. She found not just one, but two, ready and eager to get started. Two boats with women on each, four would-be fishermen who had never been on anything more than a thirty-minute ferry ride in their lives!

"Nothing doing!" I told her. "I'm not going to be tied to a couple of slow boats with landlubbers for skippers! It will be a nice cruise for them in May, but I'm not about to ride herd on them in February!"

"They're not slow boats," she explained patiently. "They are both faster than the *Tyke*, and both the women said they'd be glad to have you eat with them in return for the piloting. I'd feel so much better about you if I knew you were having decent meals, at least until you get to Alaska."

That's a woman for you. She knew, when she promised two total strangers I'd invite them to play follow-the-leader all the way to Ketchikan, that she had one argument I could not resist. I detest cooking. When a man is alone on his boat, he gets mighty familiar with a can-opener. But the last time I'd traveled with strangers, I swore there'd never be another such adventure for me. Running with experienced partners is one thing. Taking the responsibility for people who know nothing about navigation is another thing, and one that can have serious complications. It is all right for partner boats to split up so long as neither is having trouble, but to go off and leave a greenhorn is about as bad as hit-and-run driving. Once you hook up with a greenhorn, you're stuck until you get wherever you're going.

As it turned out, the couples on the *Evening Star* and the *Shag* were my kind of folks. They had the same interests and ideas. They were the type I'd associate with and enjoy under most circumstances, and they averaged only a few years younger than I. Mature, sensible folks—sensible, that is, about everything but fishing.

Dan and Mary Dobson, proud new owners of the *Evening Star*, had converted her from a surplus Coast Guard fifty-footer. A fast, sturdy sea boat with quarters for six, she was not designed for fishing, and she was a gas hog with her twin engines. The Rays, Martha and Sonny, had the *Shag*. A craft with beautiful lines, she had started life as a windjammer. Now, after several conversions and many years, she was reduced like a broken-down thoroughbred on a garbage cart, to a glamorless old fish boat.

I found one thing to be thankful for. Dobson was a mechanic— a calling most useful on a gas boat, and one with which he should have stayed. Sonny Ray was not mis-nicknamed. He was a bright, cheerful little guy with a tiny wife who is about the cutest trick I've seen in the trolling fleet. They walked around with headroom to spare under the low overhead of the *Shag*, where the rest of us had to duck and dodge.

Sonny had sold a small grocery store to finance their insanity. He'd held out enough canned goods, staples and edibles to fill every locker, cubbyhole and empty bunk on both boats. After a peek at that pile of grub and a taste of that gal's cooking, I gave up with an apology for ever having thought I didn't want their company.

We were a gay party starting out from Salmon Bay. Several carloads of friends forgot for a few moments the shackles that held them earthbound as they rode down Lake Union Canal with us on the way to the Government locks. The weather was perfect—bright and crisp, with a light northerly breeze. A wonderful send-off, for everyone except me. At the locks, where we dropped from lake level to the level of Puget Sound, I had my first demonstration of what my wife's contract had bound me to.

To unload our boisterous passengers it was necessary to come alongside a solid cement wall. I eased in, and motioned for Dan to do so astern of me. I could hear him explaining to his envious friends how easy it is to maneuver with twin screws. For a man not two months out of a machine shop, he was good, but not good enough to allow for the current that smacked him into the unyielding wall. The crash frightened Sonny off so far that I had to heave him a line, and then he came in ahead of me, headed the wrong way.

Everyone seemed to think it all part of the farewell frolic, but that kind of seamanship in calm water quenched my interest in gaiety. Then everyone shook hands and said how much they envied us. A gentle little old lady, who I later learned was Martha Ray's aunt, kept repeating how glad she was that I was going to show the others the way. I was already feeling low, but not quite low enough to tell her the truth. It was going to take a lot more than showing the way to get our little flotilla out of American waters.

The attendant at the locks was about ready to give up when we were finally lined up in the small chamber, ready for the drop to tidewater. Then they pulled the cork. The tide was low, which makes the drop its longest and transforms the confined water into a sucking whirlpool. I was on the inside, paying out the lines that hold one steady. The *Shag* and the *Evening Star* pulled loose and started on an independent little cruise. Both women were screaming. Sonny was tearing at a jumble of rope, hunting for a loose end. Dan bellowed up out of our rapidly deepening well, "Hold the water!" It was a busy little show, which the attendants and our friends seemed to find quite amusing.

The *Shag* ricocheted off the far wall and shoved the *Star* back at the *Tyke*, ripping off two fenders. When the lower gates swung slowly open, we came out like three ponies fighting for the inside rail. It was evident I was going to earn that delicious home cooking, if I lived to eat it.

It was also evident, before Seattle was lost in the smoky blur astern, that the mechanic was on the wrong boat. The *Shag* had a pair of bell-shaped cylinders that passed for her power plant. Either the maker was ashamed to put his name on it, or it had been effaced in antiquity. But when those cylinders could be persuaded to function, it was surprising how that lovely hull would slip through the water with scarce a ripple. I soon learned that the *Tyke*, with a foaming bone in her teeth, had to do better than eight knots to keep up.

The *Shag* and her skipper had one trait in common. Neither seemed to take much interest in that heap of scrap iron that was supposed to shove them up the channel. Like a family skeleton, it was never mentioned. It was hidden somewhere down in the deep bilge. I never saw it, and I have no regrets considering what happened.

My newly painted, freshly overhauled engine was the proud heart of the *Tyke*. It shared my eight-by-fourteen quarters, and its every cough and sneeze were carefully treated. I was always checking oil or gas, or planning some adjustments to show my solicitude. Not so with Sonny. I never saw him performing any of the rites. It was possible that when he gassed up he put his gas into the *Star*.

That would have been only fair. The first time the *Shag* fell behind, both Dobson and I came about to find Sonny sitting on the bow with the tow line ready.

"I told you to get some of that mica insulation for that damned make-or-break," Dan shouted before he came alongside.

"They don't make it any more," Sonny said placidly. "Don't you think it would be better to tie me on behind, and look at The Thing tonight?"

"By George, I'd ruther," Dan boomed back, and an arrangement was made that went into effect at least once daily through the rest of the voyage.

The pattern was set. With charts, tide tables, current tables, parallel rules and dividers, I set the course and took the lead. Mary steered the *Evening Star* dutifully in my wake following every little twist and turn, most of them unintentional on my part. Dan began shaping out a new piece of insulation. It takes a wizard to know what an engine needs without going near it.

At the end of the tow line the *Shag*, her stubbed-off bowsprit in the air, followed along as serenely oblivious to one form of propulsion as to another. Sonny had lashed the wheel and was below watching Martha whip up some out-of-this world surprise for the evening meal. The three boats held uniform speed and distance with Mary at the wheel of the *Star*, but as soon as Dan took over our pleasant little game of follow-the-leader was changed without warning into a breathless game of tag.

If we were in the middle of a wide channel or open reach, he would stick to me like a barnacle. In rough water, when it was necessary to keep a safe distance apart, he would crowd in the closest. When there is water in all directions except straight up, there are no dangers unless one strikes another boat. With Dan's system, I was often hard put to keep from being that other boat. But when we entered constricted passages with hidden rocks and dangerous reefs, Dan, with his greater speed, would go skylarking off around me. Most landlubbers have that mistaken feeling of safety when close to the beach where the hazards are greatest.

That first day we bowled along until Smith Island Light in the Strait of Juan de Fuca was abeam to starboard. Even though the *Star* was towing the haughty *Shag*, we were making good time. The sea was dead calm, making the crossing of the strait a pleasure. Canada's Vancouver Island, the San Juan Islands and the mainland around Bellingham fanned out before us.

We were facing the famous Inside Passage of British Columbia. Its appeal to me will never dim. Green mountains wearing fresh snowcaps close in on deep gray-green channels. Short stretches of island-studded seas make the protected fairways appreciated. The beauty, the charm, the excitement, would be increased only by sharing it with such enthusiastic first-timers as the Dobsons and the Rays. It was the beginning of their Great Adventure, a change in their way of life that, if successful, would never again allow them to return to the quiet humdrum walks. Henceforward, each day's activities would be regulated by weather and tides. Each evening's hope, a snug harbor for the night. A period of rest in the winter, but always the next season to prepare for.

Let's see. Tonight Martha had promised fried chicken. Oh, man! What that sea breeze does to one's appetite!

Smith Island abeam to starboard, the billowing reach of San Juan to port leading to the open Pacific, dead ahead Cattle Point marking the narrow entrance. My premature dreams of a pleasant passage were split wide open. The *Evening Star*, with her docile tow, had swung off on a new bearing that would lead outside the islands in the regular steamship course.

When it became apparent that Dan did not intend to swing in astern, I ran up our prearranged two-way radio signal, the pennant Baker.

"*Tyke* to *Evening Star*. Do you read?" I called as soon as the small set was warmed up.

"*Evening Star* to *Tyke*. You are loud and clear. Go ahead."

"What's the matter, Dan? Are you having trouble? Over."

"*Evening Star* back. No trouble. I just figured that is Lime Kiln Light ahead and I could get a straighter shot at it than the way you're going. Over."

"*Tyke* back. That is Lime Kiln, all right, but we don't go that way. Not if we are going to stop at Friday Harbor tonight, as planned."

"*Star* back. An old fisherman marked my chart when we were in Salmon Bay, to go around Lime Kiln Light."

Dan had asked everyone in Seattle who had ever been to Alaska for what he called "the right route." Profanity is not permitted over the air, but it would have taken more than a regulation for me to keep the air waves pure. After a few sizzling remarks indicating that I would be glad for Dan to keep right on as he was bearing until he was out of my sight forever, I cooled down a little and said, "Now listen. That light is on one side of San Juan Island, and Friday Harbor is on the other. If you are so damned good at reading charts, you should see that. About five or six miles beyond the entrance dead ahead, and we will be moored for the night."

"Oh, is Friday Harbor up that way? Well, heck, that's nothing to get sore about. Let's go that way."

"A splendid suggestion, Dan. A very good one, and you had better get on my tail and stay there because we are coming to some rocks and rips that your old fisherman may have forgotten to mark. *Tyke* off and out."

A very meek Dan followed me into Friday Harbor in time to top off our gas tanks and buy fresh meat. It was our last American port before entering Canadian waters.

Mary and Martha served dinner on the *Evening Star*, because it was the only boat with plenty of room for all of us at one sitting. The meal was worth all it had cost me. They were all so anxious to make amends that they soon had me feeling like a surly brute. We made a joke of our near parting of the ways. It's hard to stay mad when a fellow is full of fried chicken.

140

But I knew something had to be done to prevent future straying from the flock that might have serious consequences, so I attempted to hold a class in navigation. With a small-scale chart on the big chart table, I showed how we were going to pick our way through the maze of channels, around the rocks and shoals and out of dead-end roads. I explained how we would be running dangerous narrows, how the tides had to be used if we were to take advantage of the swift currents they caused. I demonstrated how the Light List described each light, preventing confusion and getting lost. I charted a course with the parallel rules on the compass rose, and showed how to steer a compass course.

Then they all came aboard the *Tyke* to see the operation of the depth finder. I used it to cinch my warning to stay exactly in my wake when in shallow water, because I could tell the exact depth at all times and so keep from going aground.

They had to know about the dangers and how to avoid them. It was intentional scare talk, but all it did was to frighten the women and take a good deal of pleasure out of their trip. My efforts paid off on several occasions when the women took over, but they were wasted on the men. Dan was the kind of person who is blinded by his own unshatterable self-confidence. Sonny, as usual, was not greatly concerned. He was content to follow. His only comment was, "You know, I think I'll get me one of them maps."

Aboard the *Star* once more, we had a hilarious game of hearts and a nightcap. They were fine folks to be with. We'd have had a grand time on a pleasure cruise—but we were fishing boats clawing our way up the Inside Passage in the shortest possible time. The time was February and the responsibility was mine.

The second day was another easy run. We moored at Boat Harbor, British Columbia, before three in the afternoon to wait for the seven o'clock slack water the following morning to run Dodd's Narrows. The owner of the float gave us permission to use it, so was invited aboard for a friendly drink. He was a twinkling-eyed old Scot, who soon had a clamming party organized.

Dan and I stayed to give the engines a little attention. Before we were through the clam-diggers returned, wet and sandy, with two buckets of fat butter clams. Our new friend, Sanderson, contributed fresh shrimp. We had potato salad, steamed clams, apple pie and coffee. It was another of what was developing into a delightful series of nightly parties. I was sorry my wife had not been well enough to make the trip. She would have enhanced the pleasure—and I could have loaned her to one of the other boats at times. She is a better navigator than half the men in the fleet.

Our party that night ended with Sanderson's telling about his rumrunning days in the States during prohibition. It must have been a paying venture, as the old boy has not done a lick since.

The next morning Dodd's Narrows was as calm as Lake Union. Ling cod fishermen from Nanaimo were dragging across the approach. The *Island Commander*, a powerful tug with a log tow, was twisting through on shortened line. With our three boats, the traffic was a bit congested. Of course Dan deserted me and passed the tug on the wrong side, but we all came through with nothing worse than an angry blast from the *Commander's* whistle.

Our course lay across Nanaimo's busy outer harbor. The girls were busy on deck with cameras. More tugs with log tows, large sawdust scows, fishing boats and two speedy little cruisers made a busy waterfront scene. Behind a steamy, unfragrant pulp mill, the lovely little village straggled up the hill. Like so many of the buildings we had seen on the inside of Vancouver Island with their steep-pitched roofs, the appearance was more Old English than modern American. It was the last good-sized town we would see before Ketchikan, five hundred miles to the northwest. Ketchikan, the Gateway to Alaska, where my responsibility of "showing the way" would be ended and once more I would be free to go my way alone.

We had intended to scoot along in wide-open Georgia Strait, and be inside Cape Mudge by nightfall. My tourist pals would have enjoyed Yaculta Village, but the weather changed our minds. A brisk northerly whipped up, sending spray over the pilothouse. That is, over the *Star* and the *Tyke*. The *Shag* lifted light as a soaring gull, gave us one glance at her clean, sharp lines, and dipped back, meeting the next comber as gracefully as a maiden slipping into her lover's arms.

The *Tyke*, built along the lines of a greyhound, will buck full throttle into heavy seas, but be covered with a swelter of flying spray. On the *Star*, solid water was slapping the large windshield, causing Dan to sound very unhappy over the radio. Sonny's vote over the air was also for hunting shelter, so I changed our course to run in behind Yellow Island.

Our radio conference ended, Dan dashed off on the new bearing, leaving Sonny and me to follow at our slower speed. It was becoming uncomfortably sloppy, but not dangerous. Our only worry was that the *Shag's* temperamental engine might want to sit this one out.

I eased up, letting Sonny take the lead so I could watch out for him. No luck! The *Shag* was already losing steerage way, and though riding better than most boats do when under way was soon dead in the water. I ran up the radio signal, to which Martha replied in her first attempt.

"Hello on the *Tyke*. Hello on the *Tyke*. Hello on the *Tyke*," she called again and again. "Why don't you answer?"

I'd have been glad to, but I could tell by the signal that she still had her transmitter open, automatically closing the receiver. At last she hung up in despair, giving me a chance to tell her how to operate her equipment.

"Sonny says everything is all right," she screamed, endeavoring to overcome her broadcasting difficulties by sheer lung power. Actually, we were close enough to shout without benefit of radio. In spite of our nasty situation, it was amusing to hear her calling to Sonny somewhere down in the old hull's bowels, telling the shrieking radio off in most unladylike terms, then in a polite tone and manner attempting to carry on a conversation with me.

"Sonny says he's changing over to battery. Mag was beginning to miss." Then in a lower tone, "I wonder if he heard me that time."

"Yes, I heard you, Martha," I said. She had never understood dual ignition, but was on good terms with battery and mag and spoke of them as two extra crew members working on opposite watches. "Tell Sonny—"

It was unnecessary to tell him anything. That old windjammer took off like a flying squirrel. Martha must have been as startled as

I was, because she was still clutching the mike and holding the transmitting button open. I could hear them as well as if I were in the cabin with them, and so could everyone else tuned in on small-boat frequency.

"I don't know what I did," said Sonny, his voice shrill and breathless. "Maybe I forgot to shut off mag when I turned on battery. I'll go back and see."

"Don't you dare go leave me!" Poor little Martha was bawling now, and doing a bang-up job of it. "Here! Ask Al what to do!"

"Let her rattle, Sonny," I howled as their signal went off. "Head for that point where Dan is, and shut 'er off when you get into calm water. I'll come alongside then and take you on in, but don't dare shut off anything now!"

I poured the coal to my bouncing baby, but came in a poor third. The *Evening Star* was at anchor, and Sonny was fast to her, standing ready to take my lines. Dan was nowhere in sight.

"He's lying down," Mary said. "That milk we had on the cereal this morning must have been sour. Kinda' upset his stomach."

"That kind of milk sweetens up as soon as you get into quiet water," I told her. "See if he doesn't feel better now. We can't lay here."

Mary's usually neat, shining galley was a shambles. Broken glass, dishes, food and books were well garnished with the contents of the big coffee pot. Unquenchable Mary stood in the center of it, laughing.

"You should have heard Dan moan when the coffee pot landed!" Mary moaned to mimic him. Her hearty laughter soon had us all relaxed and laughing with her. "Didn't I do pretty well to get her in and anchored?" she asked me.

"Aw, I told you how," came a voice from one of the bunks, and we could hear the springs creaking as Dan rolled out. "By golly, you'd laugh if a man was dying."

The shamefaced grin with which Dan faced us, and Mary's recounting of the coffee pot's breaking, turned our threatened disaster into a hilarious comedy. Dan soon had battery and mag on speaking terms again. The women, giggling like two girls on a school picnic, soon had the galley cleaned up. The lockers on the *Shag* were built for heavy weather, and I'd long ago learned to keep everything shipshape.

In the landlocked channel behind Yellow Island, we were able to leave the three vessels lashed together and steam up to Comox three abreast.

"Just like a fat woman with two half-witted kids hanging onto her," Mary said.

It is an interesting sixteen miles, made more so by the new traveling arrangement. The two slower boats hung back sulkily on their spring lines as we all enjoyed the scenery and Mary's witticisms in the *Star's* roomy pilothouse.

The morning of the fourth day out, leaving Comox, we had to cross a very shallow bar three miles wide to get back into the Strait of Georgia. I was worried. If Dan made just one ill-advised dash, he would be high and dry. Inadvertently, Martha came up with the solution.

"It's such a nice, quiet day," she said. "Why not tie together again? Then we can all watch the depth finder hunt for the deep places."

It was perfect. I had them, secured on either side of me, slow down until I held all the steerageway on the *Tyke*. With a distinct range-marker cut through timber on a distant hillside dead astern, following channel spar buoys and watching the fathometer, we couldn't lose. The girls sat on the deck singing "When We Cross the Bar," Dan stood in front of the "snooper" like an old-time sailor heaving the lead line, and Sonny smiled his friendly little smile, happy to be along.

We could see all the water traffic from the broad reach of the straits converging on Cape Mudge, the beginning of Discovery Passage and still six miles from dreaded Seymour Narrows. Tug boats, fishing craft, steamers, tankers, yachts and small cruisers all plan their schedules to match the few moments of slack water in the narrows, when the tides change directions.

The feature about Seymour Narrows that makes it more dangerous than others is Ripple Rock, near the center, that covers at high water. Even if the ship can buck the current's peak velocity of twelve knots, control is uncertain with whirlpools drawing toward that deadly rock. The United States Coast Pilot says in part, "Such disasters have occurred that the United States Steamship Inspection Service has ruled that a master attempting to navigate a vessel through Seymour Narrows at other times than slack water, or nearly slack, is guilty of unskillfullness."

As we rounded the last point from the south into Seymour Narrows proper, a small inter-island freighter entered from the north. Close quarters alone, too close for company.

To stay as far as possible from Ripple Rock, I hugged Maude Island on my starboard. The freighter hugged it too. The Rules of the Road gave me the shoreline, but the oncoming skipper gave no sign that he intended to recognize my rights. I was so close I could have stepped ashore without getting my feet wet before I could see that the freighter was in a rip which would lead him out into the channel before we crashed.

Here was something on which I had not coached Dan and Sonny. It was nip and tuck, but I could see we would be clear. Dan, crowding my stern, couldn't. He put the wheel hard over for midstream at the same time as the freighter swung out to avoid us, blasting out a starboard crossing signal which didn't mean a thing to Dan. He opened both engines and zoomed under the stranger's bow by a whisker, of course passing on the wrong side and heading straight for unseen Ripple Rock!

It was high tide, which leaves only a large whirling saucer to show the location of the wicked rock. The startled *Evening Star* was in this saucer and around it three times in nothing flat. Dan, after clearing the other boat, had cut his engines in panic when he saw where he was. The captain of the freighter was warbling over the radio but I had no time for the squawk box as I swung out to get a line on the trapped boat.

About then Dan came to—or Mary took over. I'm sure I saw her at the wheel. Sonny had enough sense to hold his course, and was slipping up the shoreline where we all should have been. The radio was really squawking now, with Dan and Martha competing against the Canadian all on the same frequency. The current was making us fast. My recollections are confused. I remember cursing our late start, and praying that the *Shag* would keep out of the way. The *Tyke* was keeping me busy, taking the accelerating current broadside. She heeled over until I had to ease up and swing away from the *Star* and just in time.

146

Dan must have restarted the engines with the throttles wide open, because the *Star* exploded out of the frothing whirlpool full bore and headed straight at me!

Poor old *Tyke*. That was the second time in a few moments that an oncoming craft had been racing at her. Fright gave her wings. We roared on through the narrows. I was still ahead, but not leading. All I was trying to do was keep from being rammed. If I'd been fast enough, I'd have continued all the way to Ketchikan without stopping. Mad, shaken and badly frightened, I was ready to dissolve the partnership.

In the smooth water of the wider channel, it was Mary again who picked up the pieces and mended a badly cracked relationship. Danger and excitement stimulated her to the point of intoxication. She came out on deck laughing and shouted, "He did it again! He broke the coffee pot! We'd have been fishing years ago if I'd have known it was this much fun. Let's tie together and have a snack."

How could a man stay mad at a woman like that? I couldn't blame Dan much, either. It certainly had looked as if the guy on the freighter intended to use our side of the road. And another thing. The night before, when Mary was high with excitement, the cooking was even better than usual. I had a hollow feeling in my stomach that was going to be mighty hard to fill.

That night we had a hoedown at Rock Bay, a little logging camp. Mary and Martha had us all fed by the time we docked. Sonny surprised me by breaking out a first class accordion and playing it as it should be played. The music brought the camp's entire population down to the dock with an invitation to bring the accordion up to an old store building where we could dance. There were two bright old French biddies, a pert young Canadian bride and three native women married to white loggers. The men were a rough, hearty group with a strong English flavor.

They had two guitars and a fiddle, which every one of those Limies could play. We had music, dancing, feats of strength and individual jigs. Martha sang some real old ballads that had half the men and all the women wiping their eyes. After the sport, we were all herded into the mess hall. If the food on those tables was any indication, Canada is surely a land of plenty. When I crawled into my bunk I didn't care whether we ever reached Alaska.

It was a cold, cruel duty to roll out before daylight to pick up the tide, or rather have the tide pick us up. The mooring lines were frozen into stiff, clutching fingers, reluctant to turn us loose in the tiny, ice-crusted bay. The swift tidal current, which kept the ice from forming in the channel, carried us past Helmcken Island, Salmon River, Cracroft Light, around Ella Point and into Alert Bay.

Snuggled back in the cove on the starboard side is the town and cannery. On the port, an Indian village is splattered along the beach. What I think is the best collection of totem poles on the coast brought out the cameras. My veto of a layover brought threats of a reduction in my pie ration. I was anxious, however, to reach the approach to Queen Charlotte Sound the next day, to take advantage of the fine traveling weather we were having.

Queen Charlotte is the largest body of open water to be crossed on the regular steamship lane between Seattle and Ketchikan. There is a rocky back-channel bypass that I have never traveled. The Coast Pilot warns that local knowledge is necessary for boats using it, and I was not about to gain that knowledge with my undisciplined convoy.

At that, the delay was enough to force us into Hardy Bay, about one hour's run from the jumping-off harbor we should have reached. Our run for the day logged only seventy-four nautical miles, compared to eighty-four and a half for the previous day.

To the Dobsons and the Rays, accustomed to car mileage, marine travel was ridiculously slow. Logging eight knots, with twelve hours of daylight, we should have done about a hundred, but we seldom did. Weather-constricted passages, adverse currents, breakdowns and other delays brought our average down to fifty-three. The passenger liners, running day and night, make it in three days. I have made it in a small boat in six days, cheating a little on both ends of the daylight hours. Many, attempting the run in winter, have taken as long as six weeks, being laid up most of the time waiting for weather.

At dinner that night the threat to my pie ration was rescinded. With the second wedge and a big mug of black coffee, I was ready to discuss the bugaboo of the Inside Passage—Queen Charlotte Sound. It can be a nasty four-hour stretch. After you poke your nose around Scarlett Point, the Inside Passage becomes a one-sided arrangement. It still exists on your starboard, but on the port there is nothing between you and Japan.

It was agreed that if any boat found the going too tough, we would all put back. As our good weather was due for a change any time, I did everything to convince the others we must get across while we had a chance. The one condition I never thought to talk over added a new game to our collection—ring-around-the-rosie. Although I never have enjoyed that game especially, I must admit that this time Dan chose a spot where there was plenty of room in which to play.

The morning promised an easy crossing. Clear, calm, cold, with just a dusting of snow sometime during the night. Every evergreen on little Pine Island was an individually decorated Christmas tree. Cape Calvert, where our passage would once more be two-sided, looked deceivingly close. Also deceiving was the ground swell. A radio conference showed us all confident of an uneventful little outing.

"That's Cape Calvert just over the boat we can see dead ahead," I called.

"Nothing to it," reported the *Evening Star*. "Is that what everybody makes such a fuss about?"

"That boat is having trouble," declared Martha. "I can see them running around on deck." Martha was working the binoculars, as usual.

"No," I explained, "it's a halibut boat, most likely working long line for cod. Slow down when we pass, and you might be able to see them landing a fish. I think they're hauling now."

We slowed down, all right, and saw not only a fish landed, but we also saw Canadian fishermen looking as bugeyed as the fish flopping on their decks. While watching them shake off three good-sized dogfish, I forgot to keep track of my following. When I remembered, I saw them headed for Seattle with the radio signal flying. I came about the fishing boat in a big circle, squalling for the reason for the about-face.

"Old busted coffee pot's milk has gone sour again," Mary explained.

"What the heck," I pleaded. "We're nearly half way. It's as easy to wade on through this puddle as it is to go back now. Is Dan where he can hear me?"

"Where he is, with that hardwood collar around his neck, I doubt if he can hear anything," Mary replied, seeming to enjoy our new game.

"Listen, Mary," I begged. "Don't say anything. Just come around in a big circle so Dan won't feel it. Remember how it was at Yellow Island? He'll be fine as soon as we're out of this swell. I'll leave the radio on so you can call me any time."

Around the bewildered Canadians we raced again. Their white-clad cook joined the crew on deck to watch the new American pastime. Dan's voice came through above the engine noise and static. "I don't think I can make it, Al. I've been poisoned. I've got to get back to that doctor at Hardy." And back he went.

The *Shag* was tired of the game, so lay to by the codders to take pictures.

"Okay, Dan," I answered, trying to sound sympathetic. "The best thing for you to do is get flat on your back and stay there. Mary can take her in."

In a few minutes Mary was back on the radio.

"Darn Martha!" she said, "over there flirting with those Canucks, and I was just starting to get acquainted!" Then, in a lower tone, "Okay, Skipper, here we go again. I think my busted coffee pot is down for the count this time. Poor guy, I'll bet he's twenty pounds lighter."

Once more we tore past the floating grandstand, this time sucking the *Shag* along in our wake, and not a peep came from anyone until we were moored in Namu Harbor six hours later. It was early to lay up, but with Seymour Narrows and Queen Charlotte Sound both behind us, a celebration was in order. While Sonny and I were making all secure for the night, the girls whipped up some drinks. Dan was still in the sack.

"Come on up," his spouse called. "There's no doctor, but we have some medicine that'll make you well."

I also felt better. One day nearer the finish line, and our two worst obstacles conquered.

The crossing of Milbanke Sound next day went off like well-ordered drill. Dan hit his bunk before anything started, and made the startling discovery that a man can be seasick and still live. It was our best day—ninety-and-one-half miles. Finlayson Channel,

Klemtu Passage and Graham Reach all seemed like following up a mighty river, instead of traveling salt-water arms of a very unpacific old Pacific Ocean.

Our mooring that night provided the most eerie experience of the entire nightmare. I was doubtful about broken-off pilings in deserted Swanson Bay. To anchor on top of one would be a great deal like the old boy in "The Skeleton in Armor," the part that goes, "There fell I upon my sword."

It was dark, but moonlight enough for visibility, so we decided to go on to Butedale. The moon led us along a bright, narrow path between the dark shadows of steep banks. Tied together, we floated on that silver ribbon, one man at the center boat's wheel and one on the bow to watch for drift and deadheads. The girls, wrapped in blankets, sat on deck singing softly to the music from Sonny's squeeze box.

Engines always purr along more easily and quietly at night. It was impossible to believe that somewhere people were worried about atom bombs and the price of coffee. The spotlight picked up a white spot in the dark shadows. It was a gull's ghost. No real gull could be that white, nor as much a part of the night, as he wheeled and joined our enchanted flight.

More gulls, without a sound, came from nowhere to greet us— bits of phantom white drifting with us. There was a luminescence not borrowed from the cold, haughty moon. It developed into a distinct glow from a snowy cloud in the passage ahead. No fog should shine like that.

The notes of the music hurried ahead and were swallowed in the billowy whiteness. No one spoke. No questions were needed. We were no longer earthbound. Wafted along the moonbeam trail we were about to become a part of—

The awakening was unbearable. A stench engulfed us, so terrible it was sticky to the touch. Foul and clammy it had us all gasping.

"I never thought fairyland would smell like this!" one of the women muttered.

"Shut off the engines! I'm going blind," roared Dan.

I knew what it was, and where we were, but still it was difficult to come back to earth. "It's all right, folks. We've reached Butedale. That's the stink plant—herring reduction. I guess they must be working the night shift."

They were. Lit up like a ball park, they were going full blast. Our snowy cloud was the putrid steam, drifting before the bright lights, made from the water content of thousands of unfortunate herring.

"Oh, we can't stay here!" Martha wailed. "It'll rot the boats, and we'll all drown in that filthy water!"

"As soon as your smeller gives up, you'll forget all about it," I said. Unbelievable as my statement was, it was no stranger than the scene before us. Here, in the midst of a wilderness where nothing more exciting than a belligerent sea lion or a startled deer was expected, was a small stain of man's greed and pollution. A sturdy, modern plant, a store, marine gas stations and dwellings, with a cascading mountain stream in the backdrop. Large seine boats, their decks awash because of the slimy loads in their holds, were waiting their turns to regurgitate their contributions. Electric fork trucks scurried about. Steam hissed, machinery clanked, and one of our finest foods was being reduced to meal. Hurry, hurry, hurry! The season is short and every minute counts. Yes sir, that's a stink plant, and right in God's lap. Rich, fat herring for seven dollars and fifty cents a ton!

The following morning, our ninth day, found us creeping up the last long narrow reach of the Inside Passage—Grenville Channel. Our start was late because we had waited for good light to take pictures of Butedale. It was a day for pictures in a picture land. The coniferous jungle crowding down to the high tide mark still held a light dusting of snow. Up on the steep banks, dark green faded to solid white. In the most rugged passes the buried peaks seemed to jut out over the emerald waterway. One had to step on deck, out from overhead, to see them.

As we neared Morning Point I could see a piece of dark drift moving across the channel. Where currents can run only up or down, such a phenomenon called for investigation. Hurriedly I put the glasses on it. Ah, now we would get some unusual pictures.

As soon as the other boats, strung out astern, replied to the radio signal, I called out, "Get out your cameras, girls. We've found a new playmate!"

It was a fine, big, black-tailed buck with only pads showing where last year's antlers had been. It may be only a coincidence, but

I believe we were on a regular deer crossing. A few years earlier I had intercepted a pair of yearlings in the same spot. In spite of their spindly shanks and tiny hoofs, a deer does all right as a sea-going critter. In Cordova Bay I once overtook one a good three miles from shore. Their thick, heavy pelts give them the appearance of being supported by dun-colored life jackets.

This one was as much interested in us as we were in him. When I cut across his bow, he disengaged his clutch and quietly looked us over.

The other two boats bearing down on us with the women screeching on deck more than satisfied his curiosity, but didn't make him retreat. He was headed for the western shore, and that was where he intended to go. When he attempted to swim around my bow, I speeded up and held him for the clicking cameras. He turned to go astern, so I kicked into reverse and cut him off again.

"Don't hurt him, the poor thing!" There was no doubt about Martha's being on his side.

"Hurt him, heck!" I said. "The old boy is so mad he's going to ram me!"

The *Tyke's* well deck in his course was no obstacle to that big fellow. Up and out he heaved. With a clatter of hoofs he was on deck. Cameras were forgotten. Everyone else was more excited than my new crew member. Dan yelled to get a rope on him. Sonny suggested a little impromptu bull-dogging. Martha was afraid the "sweet thing" would break a leg. Mary was more practical. "Don't just stand there," she scolded. "Get him a towel!"

I was the one who needed a towel. With an all-out shake like a wet spaniel, my channel-swimmer sprayed water in every direction. I thought someone had turned a fire hose on me. That was the end of the show. Light as thistledown, the deer cleared the low bulwark and continued his swim. Lashed together with the "old fat lady" in the middle, we also continued. Mary made hot coffee while I went below to change clothes. I don't understand how a deer could carry that much water.

We anchored out that night for the first time on the trip. Every other stop had been at a dock or a float. We planned an early start next morning that would enable us to complete Grenville Channel, run up Chatham Sound past the turn-off to Prince Rupert and reach Alaskan waters by nightfall.

The overdue southeaster caught us in the approach to the sound and forced us into Lewis Anchorage. There is a half-deserted Indian village in the anchorage. We had dropped the hook close to one shack that had a thin streamer of smoke attached, although there was no other evidence of life. Before we could get the fenders adjusted, Martha had her powerful binoculars out prying into the homelife of the Indians.

Suddenly she screamed, "Al, come quick! There's a little Indian dog drowning. It went down right back of the boat! Hurry, get a rowboat!"

"Well, for gosh sakes, Martha," I said, "haven't you noticed those hair seals before?"

"Well, yes," she said doubtfully. "Sonny told me about the hair seals. But this was a little puppy—I think."

"It was a pup, all right. A seal pup. You watch closely. It'll come up again. They're curious. They make cute pets, but they're like a land otter. They sure mess things up."

I had forgotten that only a month ago none of these people had ever been on salt water. What would happen to them after their safe delivery to Ketchikan? An experienced fisherman faces many unavoidable risks—enough, without those caused by sheer ignorance. Yes, I was carrying a heavy responsibility that I would be glad to shed once we tied up in Thomas Basin.

We had only about a hundred miles left, and were able to make it in easy days. Torrential rain knocked down the southeast swell, but with it astern we really rolled. It was sloppy crossing Dixon Entrance, but I was now in home waters. Without incident I led them close in the lee of Duke Island, through narrow Duck Island Passage, past Fripo Island where the bones of a wrecked halibut schooner show at low tide, and across the Mary Island flats. Up Tongass Narrows, and we were in Thomas Basin, Ketchikan's moorage, one of the best in Southeastern Alaska.

The basin was packed with evidence that the bustling little city is supported by the men who go down to the sea. Boats were tied five and six deep. Trollers, seiners, halibut boats, cruisers, work boats, barges, tugs and skiffs, all mixed together, each owner trying to get as close as possible to the floats where water and electricity are available. The best we could do was a hole where only three large seiners were moored. At that the Rays, on the outside, had to clamber over five other boats to get ashore.

We gathered then on the *Evening Star* for what I thought was to be our final celebration. We had something to celebrate. We had clawed our way up the famous Inside Passage without a scratch. I had fulfilled my contract. Now it was every man for himself.

I had them break out their charts so I could mark the best places for them to shake out their gear and get the feel of fishing protected spots with uniform bottom, where they couldn't go wrong while they learned. It was early for these places, but there was always a chance of picking up a few winter kings.

I planned to run up to Hadley, which is nearly always sloppy and has no good harbor—no place for them to start their education. All this I had still to explain to them. The women were making it tough. Now that we were near modern stores again, both were planning their shopping to include items for which I'd shown particular fondness.

"I don't see any sense in marking my map," Sonny said. "I'd rather just follow around behind you, and besides, I don't understand those maps very well anyhow."

"Well," I said, "that wouldn't work very well because I figure on making quite a run this trip, and it would be much better for both of you to start out easy. Just fish close to town until you're sure everything's working right."

"Don't worry about that," Dan said. "I can keep the wheels turning, and besides, I don't like the sound of your engine. I'm going to check it over in the morning."

The cabin was filled with promising odors from the galley. This wasn't working out the way I'd planned. It would be easier to explain the situation after we'd eaten. But before we were through eating, friends of mine had spotted the *Tyke* and were looking for me. There was coffee for everyone, and we spent the evening catching me up on the gossip of the fleet.

Then we made up gear, marked lines and visited around the basin. Somehow I never got around to make that trip to Hadley.

When the weather cleared we left town in that same one-two-three formation in which we had come. Early kings were showing up in Clover Pass, which is nice, easy fishing, so I decided to make a short trip there and help them get started. We got along so well we decided to make another trip. They caught on fast and were soon doing as well or better than I was. Soon we were all planning on going up to Cross Sound together next summer.

Yes, as I said, they sure are fine folks to travel with!

AFTERWORD:

Listening to the Voices of the Coast

by Charles Lillard

Romantic as Dian Turlon in "Daughter of the Coast" may sound, there is nothing fictional about her love. People felt that way about the coast in her day; some still did well into the 1950s. Kit Carson, who shows Edward A. Lawrence a campsite in "On the Way to Knudson Cove," was one of these people. Those of us who sat around Carson's barrel heater are not likely to forget his stories. As Lawrence says, Carson wrote for *The Alaska Sportsman*; his articles like "The Luckiest Bear in Alaska" and "Some Wolves Get Away" are still readable. Good as these written stories are, Carson only got under the skin of things when he started telling stories to an audience he could see. That's when we felt the call of the coast.

The first writers who managed to get this 'call' into their writing were the early daughters of the coast. These women were the ones who frequently found this coastal spell impossible to break, maybe because they were not supposed to know of its existence— "a woman's place is in the home" and all that entails. Barrett Willoughby was the first to break free and write. Emily Carr came later, only because she began writing so much later. The same is true of Margaret Bell.

Born in Victoria and raised in turn-of-the-century Alaska and Puget Sound, Bell returned to Southeastern (as it was called in those days) Alaska, after years in California, with one idea in mind. She wanted to write books; she did do. Small-c classics like *Watch for a Tall White Sail*, a novel for youngsters that would remain in print for 40 years, is only the best known of her numerous novels. She wrote it at Loring on Naha Bay, the place with which Eliza Scidmore had fallen in love back in 1883. "Of all the lovely spots in Alaska,"

Scidmore wrote of Naha Bay, "commend me to this little land-locked bay, where the clear green waters are stirred with the leaping of thousands of salmon, and the shores are clothed with an enchanted forest of giant pines, and the undergrowth is a tangle of ferns and salmon-berry bushes, and the ground, and every log are covered with wonderful mosses, into which the foot sinks at every splash."

It wasn't much different in 1958 when I arrived in my skiff with a case of Danish beer. Margaret was 60, I was 14; she had a library I wanted to read. Years later she told me how she'd only invited me in that afternoon because I was smoking Camels and she had hadn't had a tailor-made in two weeks. Whatever. She knew the coast and its literature: she could answer my questions; nothing else mattered. Ten minutes after we started talking, she began waving books at me. That evening she filled my packsack with books, saying, "Bring them back in the spring." Ten days later I was back, riding the cusp of a October gale. During that second visit Margaret talked long about coast writers, some of whom had been acquaintances of hers in Portland, San Francisco, Carmel.

Early on, Margaret talked about Eliza Scidmore more than anyone else, maybe because she was thinking about a book or article on Scidmore. As a writer, SCIDMORE (1856-1928) is an almost forgotten figure today; but there are reasons to remember her, just as there are to read her. Scidmore made the first of several trips to Alaska in 1883. Her first book, *Alaska, Its Southern Coast and the Sitkan Archipelago*, made up from her newspaper articles about her coastal travels in 1883 and again in 1884, was published two years later. Today we can look back and say this book is the first travel account of consequence about the Inside Passage.

In 1893 Scidmore wrote *Appleton's Guide-Book to Alaska and the Northwest Coast*, a book containing a yet-to-be-digested amount of information about the Inside Passage. As well as being an early editor and contributor to the *National Geographic*, Scidmore was the first woman on the National Geographic Society's board of managers.

There at Naha Bay, at the crumbling edges of Loring—a ghost-town memory of one of the world's largest salmon canneries—books were given to me that are in my library yet. For years

Margaret and I talked and talked; if she didn't own the books, she had read them—Marius Barbeau's *Alaska Beckons*, Ella Higginson's *Alaska*, Franz Boas's mighty *Tsimshian Mythology*, Roderick Haig-Brown's *Starbuck Valley Winter*, Archie Binns's *Headwaters* and...and.... The good and the bad were equal, so long as they were useful.

Sometimes the serendipity (Bell would have called it synchronicity) was uncanny. No sooner had she spoken of Barrett Willoughby, whom Margaret had met now and again at San Francisco literary 'do's' in the 1920s, than I found her best novel—*Spawn of the North*. It was lying forgotten in a deserted camp on Back Island, then a paradise, now a nuclear submarine base of some sort.

Barrett WILLOUGHBY was Alaska's best-known and most prolific author in the first half of the 20th century; she was also the first Alaskan to write about her home for an international audience. Among her books are the novels *Where the Sun Swings North*, *Rocking Moon*, *The Golden Totem*, and *River House*. Among her non-fiction works *Sitka* is the book about the spirit of place in Southeastern Alaska; nothing exists quite like it. Much of Willoughby's early non-fiction about the Inside Passage awaits readers who can find collections of *Sunset* and *American Magazine*.

When *Spawn of the North* appeared in 1932 the Alaskan salmon canning industry had hit the first of the many shoals that lay ahead. The Alaska Packer's cannery at Loring is a good example. After decades of over-fishing, and an almost equally long period of attempting to restock its major producer—the Naha River—the cannery went bows under a couple of times during the 1920s. After the 1930 season it sank without a sound. Its run had been a good one, but its success—the ability to pack 2600 cases a day for weeks on end—was its biggest weakness. So the bittersweet note of having reached a point of no return was a feeling shared not only by the Turlon family, but by the industry from San Francisco to the Bering Sea.

Properly, the work of Willoughby should be followed by a selection from one of Emily Carr's books, or Bell's. But such a sequence would put a kink in the direction of this anthology. We would have to turn from unexplored territory to the known for all of Carr's work is available; and turning to Bell is unprofitable for she wrote nothing for adults. Somewhere else, perhaps, the coast as seen by its earliest daughters can be followed to a conclusion.

Margaret Bell wasn't my only source of coastal lore in those days, though she certainly was the major one. Ballard Hadman lived nearby. *As the Sailor Loves the Sea*, Hadman's account of salmon trolling in Alaska, even though published as long ago as 1951, remains the most readable of the many books about trolling. Some readers would put Edith Iglauer's *Fishing with John* on the same shelf, but Hadman's zest and spontaneity are hard to best. Hadman lived on the dirt track that led from Knudson Cove to Ketchikan. In the other direction, out on Betton Island, a couple of families were logging with a small A-frame. The oldest of the two men there was Earl Judson Conkle.

He was the author of *Alaska Gold*, a collection of verse that is not as bad as expected. Writing and publishing poetry was unique in Alaska, but not, I'd later discover, in British Columbia. One day someone will collect the best coastal poetry, much of it about Puget Sound and Alaska, that was published in B.C. between WW I and the Korean War. What an aspect of the coastal consciousness—and activity—this may reveal.

Back at Knudson Cove, Kit Carson was still writing. At anchor a few yards away the Sanstroms—a father-and-son team commercial fishing out of a cruiser—spent several summers at the cove; the son, who soon bought a troller and went north, built model ships, while his father wrote for *The Saturday Evening Post*. Another person who used the cove as a jumping-off place was Emery Tobin, editor of *The Alaska Sportsman*. For years it was *the* magazine for anyone interested in the mystique of the Alaska Panhandle. There's been nothing like it since. Years later and farther south in British Columbia, Howard White would start the *Raincoast Chronicles*, which involved itself in some of the same themes as did Tobin's original magazine.

During this same time Edward A. LAWRENCE published his *Clover Passage*, which briefly enjoyed a well-deserved amount of local popularity before it was forgotten. Lawrence had fished the boat 31A990 locally in the late 1940s, and in his book he mentioned everyone who was anyone. Like so many fisherman who returned to Seattle every fall, one year Lawrence did not return. He was last known to be living in Kentucky.

Among the writers who published in *The Sportsman* was Handlogger Jackson. From him I learned of Stewart Edward

White's *Wild Geese Calling*, the fictionalized account of a family who worked their way up the Inside Passage to Alaska. Jackson had married into that family and some of the descendants lived in the Clover Pass area; later Jackson would document his own life on the coast in *Handloggers*. Reading White's novel led me in a roundabout manner to Kathrene Pinkerton.

Kathrene PINKERTON (1887-1967) and Robert, her husband, were widely known as authors of pulp fiction in the 1920s and 1930s. Between 1939 and 1941, Kathrene Pinkerton wrote *Wilderness Wife, Three's A Crew, Adventure North,* and *Two Ends to Our Shoestring;* it is on these books that her reputation as a writer rests. Some ten years later she wrote a number of juvenile novels about life along the B.C.-Alaska coast.

Pinkerton's juvenile novels were easy to find. *Hidden Harbour,* set near Juneau, was an early paperback. *Peddler's Crew* turned up in a junk store, and the others came in a batch from a stateside friend. *Three's A Crew* was nowhere to be found; nor was *Two Ends to Our Shoestring.* They turned up eventually, but long after I'd left Knudson Cove for good.

That's how it went. Slowly, books about the Inside Passage filled one shelf, then another. They were reference points, figures in a landscape like Bell herself. I would be lying to say my reading was always at some rarified or adult level. The one single book that made the difference I had read long before I met Margaret Bell. It was Archie Binns's *Sea Pup,* an affectionate and gentle book about a boy and his pet seal. Part of the book is about a trip into Puget Sound that this unlikely pair made as part of a summer vacation.

That book has been reprinted since, and like Bell's and Pinkerton's juveniles, belongs in a different type of collection than this one, but it was written proof of what a boy and a boat could do. Years later I'd buy an old inboard skiff and explore the northern San Juans as a result of finding *Sea Pup* again.

Books led to boats and back again. It was this combination that led me to British Columbia, that Canadian heart of an inland waterway that begins and ends in the United States. There I found another world of books, a literature that no one in Alaska knew anything about, just as no one in B.C. knew much about U.S. coastal literature.

M. Allerdale Grainger I already knew something of because brief portions of his *Woodsmen of the West* had appeared in Ralph W. Andrews's *Glory Days of Logging*. This was long before it was reprinted in Canada as a novel. But the *Glory Days* excerpts were all I knew. It turned out that Martin Allerdale GRAINGER (1874-1941) was born in England. He grew up in Australia, then returned home to attend Cambridge. After graduation Grainger moved to British Columbia where he spent several years odd-jobbing along the coast and further north in the Cassiar country. His one book, *Woodsmen of the West*, was written and published while Grainger was in London in 1907-1908, supposedly to pay off his creditors. There is no reason to believe this since most of what Grainger said about the book, when he said anything at all of it, is fiction. In later years his youthful activities did not fit into his middle-class picture of himself. On his return to British Columbia Grainger began his 30-year career in the province's forests, first as a civil servant, then as a businessman. Long thought to be a novel, *Woodsmen* proves, on close reading, to be an autobiographical account by an educated young man who learned the hard way what gyppo logging was all about.

Between Grainger and writers like Woollen and Farson, I rediscovered V.A. EBERHART'S "Inside Passage" in a beat-up copy of *The Alaska Sportsman* in the lounge of the Martin Inn at Ocean Falls. Later I learned he was for many years a commercial fisherman based in Issaquah, Washington. His wife, Beth Eberhart, wrote of their adventures in *A Crew of Two*.

At one time Bruce McKelvie's name was everywhere in British Columbia, and even today one cannot write history in this province without coming to terms with McKelvie's efforts. MCKELVIE (1889-1960) thought of British Columbia as the 'land of destiny' long before that phrase became popular. For many years a journalist, novelist and historian, McKelvie strove to popularize the folklore and history of the land he loved. For those interested in the early history of the Inside Passage, and more particularly how the missionaries like Sheldon Jackson saw the area, McKelvie's *Huldowget* will be of interest. It's a novel about one missionary and his problems with a shaman or medicine man. Badly dated as it is, McKelvie's details and perceptions are worth noting.

Sheldon Jackson I came to via other missionaries. On editing the memoirs of Father A.J. Brabant, the first Catholic priest to work on the outside coast of Vancouver Island, I felt that, with the exception of a few interested maritime fur traders and explorers, the missionaries were the first Europeans to record life on the coast. Curiosity led to my editing a series of other accounts written by contemporaries of Jackson's.

Sheldon JACKSON (1834-1909) graduated from the Princeton Theological Seminary in 1858 and rapidly made a name for himself. In 1877 he became the superintendent of Presbyterian missions in Alaska. By 1885 Jackson was general agent for education in Alaska. Among his many activities was the creation of a college and museum at Sitka. His writings are unknown, mainly, I suppose, because of their technical nature; what wasn't dealing with education in Alaska is, like Willoughby's articles, lost in nearly forgotten magazines. Both the man and the work deserve to be better known.

Writing *Seven Shillings a Year: The History of Vancouver Island* brought me back to one of the coast's finer writers and enigmatic characters. Negley FARSON (1890-1960) reached Vancouver Island in 1922. A noted athlete at the University of Pennsylvania, by the time Farson reached the west coast he'd worked in England and Russia, travelled widely in North America, and been wounded in the war. After two quiet years at Cowichan Lake, Farson and his wife moved to Europe where his fame as a sailor, fisherman, journalist, novelist, and adventurer continued to grow. Why did he come to Vancouver Island? To rest I suppose, but whatever the reason, we have it to thank for some of the coast's best prose. His novel, *Story of a Lake*, documents life on Cowichan Lake. In my copy of this novel someone has written in the actual names of the people Farson fictionalized in his story. No wonder certain old-timers think the long-dead Farson is afraid to return to Vancouver Island.

Lukin JOHNSTON (1888-1933) was another discovery while I was working on my Vancouver Island history. A journalist and author, Johnston joined the staff of *The Province* (Vancouver) in 1909, leaving it to edit *The Cowichan Leader* in 1911, and moving on to *The Colonist* in Victoria in 1913. After serving overseas he rejoined *The Province*, where he remained as a reporter and editor until the Southam interests sent him to London as resident correspondent.

There he wrote *Down English Lanes*, and there he was returning from an interview with Adolf Hitler when he fell overboard and drowned. Johnston was the coast's most British writer, a traveller with a eye for fetching details.

Where Woollen came from baffles me. Maybe I had some money one winter and splurged; if so it was one of my better ideas. William Watson WOOLLEN (1838-1921) practised law for 60 years in Indianapolis. Author of articles and books on law and natural history, Woollen had a considerable reputation before he turned to writing his two-volume study of Captain George Vancouver's survey of the middle portion of the Old Northwest Coast. It caused its author to make five trips to Alaska, and it was this book that would carry his name into the future; sadly, he did not live to see the book in print.

One reads on, hoping to learn the identity of LANDSMAN, who recorded his happy cruise aboard the *Mineola*; hoping likewise to learn something about Sidney R. SHELDON whose "Eighteen Feet to Alaska" appears to be the only thing he ever wrote. Too, there's always the hope of finding something new, a book or even a few pages that open a new vista or focus an old one. Ezra MEEK-ER's work is one such find. Meeker (1830-1928) wrote numerous books about life on the Oregon Trail, historical events with which he'd been associated, and at least one book on growing hops. The rough-hewn dignity and sly humour of his "Cruise" is enough to make one want to find the rest of his work.

* * *

Enough of this. There is no end to reading, just as there is no end to making books, as an Egyptian scribe complained 4000 years ago. Now it is not what is in an anthology like this that haunts me, it's what has been left out. So I start a new table of contents, reach for old notebooks with their lists of books—then laugh at myself. Like poems, anthologies are never finished, they are abandoned. There's always the next one.

ACKNOWLEDGEMENTS

EBERHART, V.A.: "Inside Passage" appeared in *The Alaska Sportsman*, November 1955, and is here reprinted courtesy of *Alaska*.

FARSON, Negley: "Saga of the Pacific Salmon" originally appeared in *Going Fishing* by Negley Farson (Country Life Ltd., 1942) and is used here courtesy of the author's son, Daniel Farson.

GRAINGER, Martin Allerdale: "The Logging Coast" is made up of chapters 2 and 3, *Woodsmen of the West* (Edward Arnold, 1908).

JACKSON, Sheldon: "A Canoe Voyage into the Tongas Country" is made up of portions of chapters 9 and 10, *Alaska, and Missions of the North Pacific Coast* by Rev. Sheldon Jackson, D.D. (Dodd, Mead & Co., 1880).

JOHNSTON, Lukin: "An Island Eden" first appeared as chapters 1 and 2, *Beyond the Rockies* by Lukin Johnston (J.M. Dent & Sons Ltd., 1929) and appears here courtesy of Derek Lukin Johnston.

LANDSMAN: "The Cruise of the *Mineola*" appeared in *Westward Ho!*, June 1908.

LAWRENCE, Edward A.: "On the Way to Knudson Cove" was originally Chapter V, "The Pass," *Clover Passage* (Caxton Printers, 1954).

MCKELVIE, Bruce: "Massacre at Ganges" and "The Salt Whisky War" were collected in *Tales of Conflict* by Bruce McKelvie (The Vancouver Daily Province, 1949) and are reprinted courtesy of Mrs. L.K. McKelvie.

MEEKER, Ezra: "A Cruise on Puget Sound" is made up of portions of chapters 4 to 8, *Pioneer Reminiscences of Puget Sound* (Lowman & Hanford, 1905).

PINKERTON, Kathrene: "Pledged to Neptune" is made up of portions of chapters 15 and 16, *Two Ends to Our Shoestring* (Harcourt, Brace & Company, 1941) and is used here courtesy of David Pinkerton Gardner, Mary Pinkerton Gardner Duffey, and William Pinkerton Gardner.

SCIDMORE, Eliza: The epigraphs used as section openers are from *Alaska* (D. Lothrop and Company, 1883).

SHELDON, Sidney R.: "Eighteen Feet to Alaska" appeared in *The Alaska Sportsman*, May 1959 and is here reprinted courtesy of *Alaska*.

WILLOUGHBY, Barrett: "Daughter of the Coast" is excerpted from *Spawn of the North* (Houghton Mifflin Company, 1932).

WOOLLEN, William Watson: "Sailing with Vancouver" is made up of extracts from pages 247-276, *The Inside Passage to Alaska* (The Arthur H. Clark Company, 1924).

Despite all effort, the editor was unable to locate Edward A. Lawrence or the heirs of Barrett Willoughby. Proper acknowledgement will be made should these authors or their heirs contact him.